ADULT and CONTINUING EDUCATION

EDUCATION

Responding to Change

ADULT and CONTINUING EDUCATION

Responding to Change

HUEY B. LONG
The University of Georgia

Teachers College, Columbia University
New York and London   1983

Published by Teachers College Press, 1234 Amsterdam Avenue,
New York, N.Y. 10027

Library of Congress Cataloging in Publication Data

Long, Huey B.
　Adult and continuing education.

　Bibliography: p.
　Includes index.
　1. Adult education—United States.　2. Continuing
education—United States.　I. Title.
LC5251.L65　1983　　　374'.973　　　83-4886

ISBN 0-8077-2742-3 (pbk.)

Grateful acknowledgment is made for permission to reprint material from the
following books:

Fred Harvey Harrington, *The Future of Adult Education: New Responsibilities of
Colleges and Universities* (San Francisco: Jossey-Bass Inc., Publishers, 1977).

F. M. Hechinger, "Forty Years of Educational Technology," in G. W. Bonham (Ed.),
The Communications Revolution and the Education of Americans (New Rochelle,
N.Y.: Council on Learning, 1980). Reprinted with permission from the Council on
Learning. Copyrighted by the Council on Learning, 271 North Avenue, New Ro-
chelle, N.Y. 10801.

Manufactured in the United States of America

88 87 86 85 84 83   1 2   3   4   5   6

95557 23

Contents

Preface

The winds of change blow upon our faces with an irregular but persistent force—sometimes it is as soft as a spring breeze, and at other times it is as fierce as a winter gale. The 1960s and 1970s have been one of those exceptional periods of significant change. There is reason to believe that the next 20 years may bring even deeper changes in our social relations, our psychological perspectives, and the applications of technology.

Even as I prepared to write on this topic, a number of developments were routinely reported in the news media. One article reported an important favorable change in employer attitudes toward older employees (Porter, 1981). Another cited the discovery of the left-handed DNA molecule (*Atlanta Journal-Constitution*, 1981). A third source reported how scientists are using "nuclear" explosions in the treatment of cancer (Kindley, 1981). This medical advance was brought close to home when an acquaintance was recently referred for such treatment. Finally, a fourth writer reported the technology of using peat as an energy source based on Ireland's lengthy experience with this fuel (Sullivan, 1981).

Almost daily we read and hear of developments we cannot fully comprehend and that we often believe will not affect us or our circle of friends. But we are brought face to face with the reality of the change when we discover its impact on a personal acquaintance. Then we realize that even some of those discoveries and developments that we consider to be "far out" have direct and significant implications for us as individuals, for our social institutions, for medical care, and for the way we live our daily lives. Within such a context, individuals and institutions are challenged to remain flexible and inquiring.

In response to, and as a consequence of, momentous changes and developments, all kinds of agencies, institutions, and organizations have become involved in providing educational programming for adults. These providers include governmental units, corporations, traditional educational institutions, religious institutions and organizations, and all kinds of consulting and voluntary arrangements from the free university to learning networks.

This book is about changes that have implications for the creative origination, conceptualization, planning, structuring, delivering, and managing of what are called educational activities and programs for adults. The purpose of the volume is to acquaint the executive, the administrator, and the program planner of diverse helping organizations, training units, and educational institutions with a framework within which changes may be identified and analyzed. Identification and analysis of sociological, psychological, and technological developments at macrolevel and microlevel should be a routine part of the educational program-planning process.

The objectives of *Adult and Continuing Education: Responding to Change* were addressed by the following procedures. First, a conceptual framework, as discussed in chapter 1, was developed. Second, over 220 publications concerning selected critical areas of change were reviewed. Third, pertinent changes were noted and discussed. It is significant that 20 to 25 percent of the items in the reference list were published in 1980 and 1981. Ten sources were published before 1960, and approximately 75 percent of all references were published after 1969.

Adult and Continuing Education is divided into ten chapters that are placed in four major divisions. Part I is a one-chapter introduction that provides a conceptual paradigm for program planning. Part II is a four-chapter unit addressing the following topics: (a) social developments, (b) psychological developments, (c) technological developments in the electronic media, and (d) technological developments in administration and education.

Part III is a three-chapter division that examines three program ideas closely associated with social and psychological developments of the 1960s and 1970s. They are programs for the aging, programs for the disadvantaged, and programs for women. The chapter on programs for women includes a discussion of the results of a recent survey of leading educational programs for women in the United States developed especially for this book. Part IV contains two chapters.

The first discusses different ways that learning is now being "certified" and describes conditions that led to this development. The concluding chapter contains some speculations about the future.

In addition, a prologue that identifies some major developments is found on page xiii. Each chapter, with the exception of chapter 1, 7, and 10, also contains an additional list of significant developments pertinent to the topic.

Acknowledgments

I am deeply indebted to Cathy Morris for her professional assistance and encouragement with this manuscript. Typing assistance, moral support, and other encouraging behaviors of Carolyn Taylor, Linda Turner, Jayne Lackey, and Pauline Heuberger are also gratefully acknowledged. Finally, the volume is dedicated to my rapidly changing family, a supportive wife and three young adult children who are so much affected and challenged by the developments in social relations, psychological perspectives, and technology noted herein.

Prologue:
Adult and Continuing
Education and Change

A great shuddering irrevocable change is overtaking American society. It has been variously described in political, economic, and technological terms. More impressively, it is also described as a new mind, a turnabout in consciousness in significant numbers of critical individuals. In short, it is a new structure that is powerful enough to initiate a radical change in our culture. Educators of adults are directly and intimately associated with this shift; it has important implications for programming strategies, procedures, and content in adult and continuing education.

When individuals consider the changes that have occurred in American society since about 1960, they can be overawed. Toffler's *Future Shock* (1970) and *Third Wave* (1980) observations are more apt today than when he first wrote them. If anything, the threat to our ability to adjust to and cope with monumental, subtle, and pervasive changes is increasing daily. The events that threaten to overwhelm us or at best confuse us directly challenge educators of adults regardless of where they practice their craft.

Religious institutions are challenged to provide learning opportunities that bring their religious doctrines to bear upon changes in such areas as new life-styles, family crises, interpersonal relationships, drug use, morality, contraception, abortion, mid-life crises and other developmental passages, the electronic church, and child care.

Business and industry must adapt to opportunities for new management styles, new data-processing potential from word processing

to budgeting analyses, new organizational structures, new relationships with labor and government, and changed concepts of the workplace. Personnel in training and development units of business are
challenged by these kinds of changes.

Voluntary organizations do not escape the impact of change
either. Staff members must learn how to develop new schedules for
voluntary workers. Attitudes toward and within voluntary organizations are also subject to changes occurring in American society.

Educational institutions of all kinds are challenged by contemporary and predicted change. They must discover new working relationships with each other and with other agencies, organizations,
and institutions. They must develop program-planning procedures
that reduce the lead time now often required from inception of a program idea to successful implementation. They must learn how to
compete at a national level and how to use the electronic media for
education and for management. *Marketing education* is a new catch-
word that represents only one change in administration and program
operations in educational institutions.

Some of the developments in American society that have implications for programming in adult and continuing education are listed
below with little or no further comment. They are provided here to
illustrate the kinds of modifications and developments that affect us.
They are as follows:

- A dramatically declining fertility rate since 1957 has created a
  larger proportion of elderly people and a smaller proportion of the
  young.
- Improved medical and health care has enlarged the population sur-
  viving to old age; in 1981 the average life-span was 73.1 years.
- Social security and pension funds will need to locate additional
  dollars to support the swelling ranks of the retired.
- Attitudes about employment, marriage, contraception, abortion,
  divorce, and family size are changing.
- Demographic profiles indicate that college enrollments will decline.
- Astounding developments in American agricultural research offer
  new ways of producing more food with less energy on smaller
  areas of land; genetic engineering and plant chemistry are two
  keys to the development.

- Strategies and technology to maintain an expanding economy with less energy are emerging.
- Knowledge of how the brain functions advances; "brain pacemakers" are used to treat patients suffering from schizophrenia and other severe mental illness; sophisticated technology such as Computed Axial Tomography (CAT) and Positron Emission Tomography (PET) is used to study the brain.
- New ways of sensory feedback help some patients regain control of body parts previously affected by stroke and other accidents.
- The workplace is becoming increasingly automatized.
- People have new expectations for workplace fulfillment.
- There are fewer production jobs and more service jobs.
- High-technology employment requires new skills.

The sources of all these changes are numerous. They reside in scientific and technological sophistication, demographic attributes, and psychological phenomena. The baby boom generation born after World War II is definitely a phenomenon to be considered for the next 40 to 50 years, perhaps longer with improved health care. Scientific and technological innovations such as test-tube babies, cloning, the space shuttle, satellite communications, and automated production lines all have potential spinoffs that are difficult to imagine. Despite our ability to predict how these developments will appear in the future, we must be prepared to provide educational solutions to some of the problems.

It is appropriate that we look to education writ large for solutions to emerging issues since education has contributed to the knowledge revolution. The revolution is leading us into the unknown through work on brain hemispheres, molecular biology, biochemistry, the genetic code, primatology and ethnology, biofeedback and altered states of consciousness, medicine and psychotherapies, archaeology and astronomy, linguistics, leadership and power, the management of business, and the governance of institutions and nations.

As demonstrated in the previous pages, important changes that pose significant challenges to programming in adult and continuing education are too numerous to be individually addressed. Therefore, the following chapters contain only some representative developments. They do not exhaust the inventory of potential events and changes that will affect programming in adult and continuing education.

It can be argued that the development of moveable type made possible the scientific and technological innovations that we contend with, and benefit from, today. Which of the new developments will have an impact similar to that of the printing press? Is the electronic computer to provide the impetus for another quantum leap? Is the most astounding development to be discovered in health care one that may extend average life expectancy to 120 years? Or will we derive the greatest impact from plant science that will solve energy and protein problems for generations to come? Despite the ultimate answer, which may not be among the above, we can be assured that we will be increasingly involved in lifelong learning. Only through persistent inquiry across the life-span will humans be able to cope with future changes.

PART I

Introduction

1 Program Developments in Adult and Continuing Education: An Overview

Because concepts of education and learning are socially based, they are likely to reflect changes in the broader society. This truism is more apparent from a historical perspective where one is able to trace the development of free and compulsory schooling and significant philosophical changes concerning educational practice. Social historians, sociologists, and educators can, from the vantage point of history, identify trends and events that seem to represent the development of new ideas and values that become translated over time into educational practice and institutional structures.

Educators of adults in the last fifth of the twentieth century find themselves in a period when reform, radicalization, innovation, and modernization are collectively challenging traditional approaches to planning educational programs for adults. Contemporary institutional behavior is usually a product of an age when learning was believed to be limited to one part of life: youth. Learning was thus perceived to be a routine activity of childhood in preparation for adulthood. Increasing pressure from all kinds of social change confronts today's adult with demands for a radical reinterpretation of learning that includes learning as a lifelong process. Simultaneously, educators of adults are challenged to recast traditional concepts of learning, its content, and processes to facilitate it. The evolution of society and the concepts of education and learning thus take on major significance for the educational planner.

Planners in adult and continuing education use the term *program* to connote the means by which they bring learners, content, and processes together. Therefore, in this chapter and in this book we are concerned with two aspects of programs designed to meet the educational needs and interests of adults. We are first concerned with the concept, definitions, and planning of educational programs. But a greater interest is in the implications of social, psychological, and technological change upon program activity. We are concerned with both of these program dimensions because they have consequences for educational activities for adults. Education is both a product and stimulator of change. Because some of the problems presented by social, psychological, and technological changes are at least partially accommodated through education, this book focuses upon some of the changes that bring about the need for continuing education and learning. The concept of program provides the vehicle to address our concerns.

It is my intent to provide a new heuristic model for program planning that is sensitive to the forces currently influencing learning and educational needs of American adults. Before I explicate the model, it is desirable, if not necessary, to briefly examine five related concepts: (a) historical characteristics of adult and continuing education, (b) philosophical concepts, (c) current program concepts, (d) current classification concepts, and (e) concepts of program planning.

HISTORICAL CHARACTERISTICS

Adult and continuing education in the United States can be characterized by a combination of five descriptors; it is creative, pragmatic, voluntary, pluralistic, and dynamic. Events or conditions related to the other three descriptors continually challenge administrators, instructors, and students of the field to use pragmatic program development strategies creatively. These five selected characteristics help to explain the constantly changing programmatic thrusts of a variety of institutions identified as sources of educational assistance and learning for adults.

CREATIVITY

Planners of educational programs for adults are challenged to be creative in their efforts to meet the needs of their projected audience. Creativity is demanded by a number of forces: competition from other activities, competition from other providers of educational services, and pragmatic, voluntary, and dynamic dimensions of participation as discussed in the following paragraphs.

PRAGMATISM

The historical pragmatic characteristic of adult and continuing education is evident on two levels: the participant and the institutional. At the participant level, the emphasis has been on learning for a specific purpose; frequently such purposes include occupational improvement, the development of a useful skill, or solution of a specific problem. The pragmatic thrust of education for adults in the United States is older than the nation. It is reflected in the volume of how-to-do-it literature (Long, 1980c) published and sold since the eighteenth century and in the efforts of Benjamin Franklin and others to change college curricula to address mercantile needs in the expanding trade of the American colonies.

The literature of adult participation in educational activities is a rich source of evidence in support of the pragmatic character of adult education. Houle's (1961) classic study identifies three distinct learning orientations: goal, activity, and learning orientations. The first two reflect a pragmatic approach to adult learning activities. Goal-oriented individuals often participate in adult education for reasons of vocational improvement. More frequently, however, they have sought general self-improvement. Houle depicts goal-oriented persons as sharing a confident acceptance of adult education as a way to solve problems or to pursue particular interests. Furthermore, they attribute similar motives to other adult learners, and their history of continuing education shows clearly that they have always tended to take courses because of their belief that they would benefit from the activity (Houle, 1961). In contrast, the activity-oriented learner is attracted by the social activity. More is said about Houle's typology in chapter 3.

Tough's (1971) research concerning adult learning projects also reveals the presence of the orientations identified by Houle. Tough says that some learning projects can be defined as efforts to gain new knowledge, insight, or understanding. Others are personal attempts to improve skill or performance, or to change attitudes or emotional reactions. An additional dimension of the adult's pragmatic approach to learning is revealed by Tough's research: People seek to learn through the use of numerous resources and through a variety of methods. Course taking and participation in formal adult education programs probably involve fewer hours of learning efforts than other methods and techniques used by adults. These other methods include independent activities using such resources as audiovisual tapes, programmed instruction, and correspondence study.

Finally, Rossing and Long (1981) indicate that the curiosity of adults about a topic seems to be based more on its potential *usefulness* than on its *novelty*.

Pragmatism is also evident at the institutional or organizational level. First, program planners usually seem to be more concerned with *how* something works than *why*. Second, since most adult education institutions are self-supporting, or are expected to generate an important percentage of the adult program budget, programs that attract and maintain participants are preferred. The difficulties of sustaining certain programs such as liberal adult education and public affairs education reflect the pragmatic approach of the potential participants, and the eventual discontinuance of such efforts is a pragmatic decision at the administrative level. Philosophically, the educator may wish to offer liberal education and public affairs programs, but until some method of financing or a sufficiently creative and attractive format is developed, the program will be constrained by pragmatic realities at both levels.

VOLUNTARISM

Historically, adult and continuing education in the United States has been a voluntary activity. Even though there are important areas where its voluntary nature is being challenged, the great bulk of the field is perceived as retaining this characteristic. The historical voluntary characteristic and current events that have contributed to mandatory continuing education are both important elements in programmatic considerations. Attention here, however, is focused on the historical voluntary dimension; the mandatory aspect is discussed later.

The voluntary aspect of adult and continuing education provides a factor that is usually missing from other kinds of education, such as public schooling and degree programs in postsecondary education, historically developed for young adults and older adolescents. Much of adult and continuing education is directly dependent upon the free choice of an adult to enroll and continue in a learning experience. Consequently, administrators and teachers are required to be more sensitive to what attracts and what retains learner participation. The planning and delivery of adult and continuing education programs are thus frequently based on learner-centered factors such as needs and expectations as determined by a variety of procedures. A sizable segment of the research in the field focuses on procedures and techniques designed to identify adult learning interests and needs. More is said about this research in chapters 2 and 6.

The traditional voluntary characteristic of adult and continuing education is intrinsically related to philosophical, social, and economic programming issues. For example, are occupational and professional continuing education programs for the personal benefit of participants, or are they for the common good? If educational participation is for personal improvement, is it the responsibility of the state to bear the primary burden of such activities? If special groups are underrepresented in the distribution of wealth and goods, and if education can redress the problem, is such education the responsibility of the state? Under what conditions, if any, should an adult be required to return to some kind of schooling experience?

PLURALISM

The pluralistic characteristic of adult and continuing education is manifested in several ways. First, the audience is pluralistic. There is no *one* audience for all of adult education. Second, the institutions and organizations providing adult education are numerous and reflect diverse missions and sponsorships. Third, there are several recognized philosophies of adult education. Fourth, the different efforts to conceptualize and organize discussions of programs in adult education reflect the multidimensional character of the field.

Not only has the pluralistic nature of adult education contributed to difficulties in communication within and about the field, but it has also tended to camouflage the field sufficiently to prevent its parameters from becoming distinct. Hence, the number of participants annually involved is a debatable point. There is also a lack of clarity concerning the institutions and activities that are included. The identity problem has contributed to descriptions of the field as "marginal" and "peripheral." There is no one voice that can speak for all of adult education.

Discussions of programs and practices, functions, institutions, program areas, and analytic models later in this chapter further explicate the concept of the pluralistic attributes characteristic of the field.

DYNAMISM

Adult education, at least in part, derives its dynamic attribute from its responsiveness to change. Harrington (1977) has observed that adult learners are at the center of today's most interesting innovations in higher education, including credit for learning through life experience, credit by examination, drop-out and drop-in arrangements, special degrees for adults, weekend classes, and all kinds of nontraditional experiments.

Since 1965, for example, a number of changes in adult education have been noted. Harrington says of the period between 1965 and the early 1970s:

> One might think there was no energy left to consider the educational needs of older citizens. Yet these years were the best ever for post-secondary adult education in the United States, both at the elitist and lower-income levels. Credit and noncredit offerings, often divorced in previous periods, seemed to fit together better than before, as did classroom and out-of-classroom activity. Technological improvements make going back to school more interesting, as did experiments with credit for life experience, courses by newspaper and television, learning contracts, special degrees for adults, continuing education units, universities without walls, and learning center support for external credit students. Even more important was the increase in financial support from government and from the private sector. (1977, pp. 24–25)

Some of these developments are discussed in more detail in Part IV. Because of their flexibility, many adult education organizations can experiment with new or different target audiences, topics, and delivery processes more readily than can traditional parts of the educational system. Thus, innovations with distance learning, programs for special populations, and the use of new or different ways of relating people and content are frequently identified first in the field of adult education. After their validity has been shown, it is not unusual for the innovations to be assimilated into other educational structures. Consequently, adult education personnel quite frequently develop programs in one area and leave them for the less adventuresome while going to new program topics, audiences, or delivery systems. Social change and critical social incidents also stimulate new programs and simultaneously displace existing ones. Even a major entertainment epic such as the TV movie "Roots" may stimulate a previously moribund area, as happened with genealogy.

In addition to the historical characteristics of creativity, pragmatism, voluntarism, pluralism, and dynamism, other forces influence program development. For example, philosophical issues and positions have both obvious and subtle influences upon program ideas and structure. It should be axiomatic that educational programs reflect the philosophical orientations of institutions and their program planners. This simple observation is seldom noted in the literature of program planning and development. Because of such oversight, it is desirable to state the obvious here.

PHILOSOPHICAL REFLECTIONS

Adult education programs and their evolvement tend to reflect particular philosophical orientations concerning humanity, learner needs, purposes of education, and institutional mission. Elias and Merriam (1980) have provided a classification of adult education philosophies that contain six types: (a) liberal, (b) progressive, (c) behavioristic, (d) humanistic, (e) radical, and (f) analytical. Table 1.1 illustrates activities for five of these types of adult education.

It seems logical to assume that the process of planning and developing programs is guided both by theory and philosophy. First, it appears that one's philosophy is associated with the selection of a program development theory or process. The process is then continuously informed by philosophical values. Interpretation of social is-

TABLE 1.1:   Program Areas and Practices Classified According to Five
             Philosophies of Adult Education

Liberal	Progressive	Behavioristic	Humanistic	Radical
Great Books	Americanization Education	Competency-based Education	Group Dynamics	Freedom Schools
	English as a Second Language	Teacher Education	Group Relations Training	Free Schools
	Community School Movement	Programmed Instruction	Group Processes	Freire's Approach to Adult Literacy Education
			Sensitivity Workshops	
			Self-Directed Learning	

Source: Elias & Merriam, *Philosophical foundations of adult education* (Huntington, N.Y.: Kreiger, 1980).

sues and events is influenced by one's philosophy; similarly, the identification of an educational need and the selection of procedures to satisfy the need are all constrained by the general and educational philosophies of the program planner. For example, adult educators whose philosophies place them in the center of the liberal arts tradition are particularly challenged in the planning of a program designed to address the occupational function. Another example concerns educators who subscribe to the radical philosophy of adult education, as defined by Elias and Merriam (1980). These individuals' interpretations of educational need and selection of content and learning activities would be quite different from the same activities conducted by humanistically or behavioristically oriented educators.

CURRENT PROGRAM CONCEPTS

Unlike more traditional kinds of education, adult and continuing education can respond flexibly to the needs and interests of potential learners. Part of this flexibility resides in the structural and programmatic elements of agencies and organizations in the field. The concept of "program" seems to be one of the critical components of responsiveness. The construct provides educational planners with a means for timely analysis, planning, and development that is often missing in such concepts as curriculum. Therefore, program development in adult and continuing education is a basic activity. The entire adult education enterprise is dependent upon creation and delivery of activities and programs. Yet, the process by which educational programs for adults come into being and mature has yet to be adequately conceptualized and communicated. Communication is further complicated by the definitional problems inherent in the term *program*. Two decades ago Thomas (1964) illustrated the difficulty when he noted no term or idea throughout adult education is so widely used, nor quite so elusive in precise meaning. The term *program* is used in adult education with great license and with limited efforts to require that people agree completely on its use. Some of the elements of a program that may be more commonly accepted are: (a) it is an activity, (b) it has order and continuity, (c) it includes more than one item or event, (d) it includes educational objectives, and (e) events within the activity are related to every other event. Thomas suggests that a program may be an adult education term for what may be otherwise called a course, in the sense of a course of studies. There is more than a question of semantics involved with this idea. For example, the implication is that it is possible to have a course of study with no students in it, but it is impossible to have a program without participants (Thomas, 1964).

An educational program for adults, by necessity, must have an educational objective; otherwise the activity should be labeled as entertainment or another more appropriate term. *Program* as used to define merely a plan of action or a scheme to guide further behavior is not consistent with an educational purpose. *Program* then, as used here, is a specific situation (environment, content, learning activities, and so forth) for learning.

Thus far the discussion has identified some more or less commonly accepted elements that qualify an activity to be called an adult education program. Furthermore, Brunner et al. (1959) suggest that *program* may refer to three distinctive categories of educational activities when applied to three selected social or organizational levels. The concept they propose becomes clearer when approached in an inverse order from the one they use.

1. Activity level. *Program* may refer to one activity, such as an educational activity designed to teach adults how to prepare an income tax return.
2. Institution. *Program* may refer to all the educational activities designed for adults, for example, occupational, liberal education or hobby and craft.
3. Community. *Program* refers to the totality of all educational activities designed for adults by all institutions in the community.

Through the use of analytic philosophy techniques, Schwertz (1972) examined the literature of adult education to derive the major connotations of "program." He concludes that the term is used in ordinary language and in adult education literature in five different ways: (a) in the sense of a system (organization), (b) as a verb in the sense of a process of planning, (c) in the sense of a plan, (d) in the sense of a document, and (e) in the sense of performance (activity).

CURRENT CLASSIFICATION CONCEPTS

Assuming that the historical characteristics of educational programs for adults as previously discussed in this chapter are accurate and useful, we are yet confronted with questions about how to classify and describe educational programs according to other dimensions.

FUNCTIONS

Fifty years ago Bryson provided a useful typology of the functions of adult and continuing education. He said the field has five functions: remedial, relational, occupational, liberal education, and political education. While the range of programs by content and specialty has increased since Bryson's work and the number of institutions providing adult education services continues to expand, his historical typology seems to persist. Thus, his conceptualization remains useful for the purpose of identifying the various functions of diverse activities provided for distinctive populations.

Bryson observed, "An educational activity can be considered in terms of function, of agency, or of subject matter. One can try to understand it by what it tries to do, or by the institutions which carry on the programs, or by the content of its teaching. It can be approached in still other ways, of course, such as by describing its clientele" (1936, p. 29). Even in 1936, analysis of adult and continuing education was complicated, according to Bryson, by the rapidly changing character of the field. Thus, he tentatively suggested that adult and continuing education may be divided into five functions that he perceived as having one purpose, "the enlargement of the personality and the quickening of life" (p. 29). He added, "The deeper we go into the motives of mature men and women who are setting out to educate themselves, the more we are convinced that this fundamental motive, self-improvement, expresses itself in a thousand different ways but remains always the same" (pp. 29–30).

Boyle (1981) has developed a concept of functional program types. His scheme defines the following three types of programs in adult and continuing education: (a) developmental, (b) institutional, and (c) informational. According to Boyle, these three program types differ on a number of dimensions such as primary goal, source of objectives, use of knowledge, involvement of the learner, role of the programmer, and standards of effectiveness. For example, the primary goal of the developmental program type is to define and resolve personal, group, or social problems whereas institutional programs are primarily concerned with the growth and development of basic skills, abilities, knowledge, and competencies. Finally, according to Boyle's typology, the primary goal of informational programs is to provide for an exchange of information.

PROGRAM AREAS

A variety of schemata are available for identifying and classifying programs by "areas." The 1960 and 1970 editions of the *Handbook of Adult Education* (Knowles, 1960; Smith, Aker, & Kidd, 1970) provide examples of program typologies as does the work of Boone et al. (1980). As the following list (Lord, 1980) shows, the University of Georgia Center for Continuing Education has adopted a multidimensional system based on five major subject matter or content dimensions. Each of the five program classifications is further divided into four or more subareas:

1. Problems and Issues of Society
    1.01   Health and Safety
    1.02   Human Relations and Communications
    1.03   Education
    1.04   Government
    1.05   Business
    1.06   Law and Law Enforcement
    1.07   Community Development
    1.08   Aging
    1.09   Social Change
    1.10   Environment
    1.11   Agricultural and Food Production
2. Subjects of Personal Interest
    2.01   Leisure Time Activities
    2.02   Cultural Enrichment
    2.03   Expanding Knowledge About the World and Its People
    2.04   Civic and Economic Understanding
3. Skills and/or Knowledge for Occupational Improvement
    3.01   Professions
    3.02   Business and Industry
    3.03   Government
    3.04   Education
    3.05   Law and Law Enforcement
    3.06   Clerical
    3.07   Trades and Technologies
    3.08   Agriculture and Food Production
    3.09   Social Services
4. Subjects Related to Intellectual Skills Development
    4.01   Reading
    4.02   Writing
    4.03   Language
    4.04   Mathematics
    4.05   Critical and Creative Thinking
    4.06   Listening
5. Subjects Related to Personal Life Problems and Demands
    5.01   Finance
    5.02   Foods and Nutrition
    5.03   Family Living
    5.04   Child Development
    5.05   Health and Safety
    5.06   Personal Assessment
    5.07   Consumer Understanding

A review of different historical periods reveals a dynamic aspect to program trends even though the functions of the programs retain a generic similarity across the periods. According to Long (1976), three major program areas are clearly identifiable in the colonial period. They are apprenticeship education, public lectures, and evening schools. The number and range of institutions and sponsors gradually expanded over the last two hundred years. It is noteworthy that the basic program areas addressed several of the functions of adult and continuing education as identified by Bryson; apprenticeship education had an occupational function; public lectures addressed the liberal education, occupational, relational, and political functions; and evening schools usually were designed to serve the remedial or occupational function and perhaps occasionally the liberal education function.

Program areas, however, have taken on different forms and structure while obtaining new titles; at the same time, historical generic functions have been maintained. For example, it seems possible to include continuing professional education in the occupational function although Bryson did not devote much attention to the topic, except in this passing remark:

> It would be theoretically justifiable to consider under the heading of occupational education all the activities of professional societies of physicians, lawyers, bankers, and others, which provide apprenticeship training for their junior members and advanced study for practitioners. These are as much adult education as anything, and they are of very ancient standing. They do not appear to require any special consideration here, however, since in the first place, they have well-established ways of accomplishing their purposes, innocent for the most part of any formal method, and since they do not ask either public interest or public support. (1936, p. 36)

INSTITUTIONS

The literature of the field also identifies adult and continuing education activities via institutionally structured procedures. The complexity of society is matched by an expanding range of specialized social units such as agencies, institutions, and organizations that provide educational opportunities for adults. Liveright's (1968) list of learning sources for adults is a short one compared with that of Peterson (1979). Liveright lists

1. Established educational institutions
2. Industry and business

3. Labor
4. Voluntary associations
5. Church and religious organizations
6. Health organizations
7. Museums, art galleries, and performing arts institutions

Peterson's (1979) classification system is revealed through studying table 1.2.

Educational planners may thus discuss programs of adult and continuing education from at least three different perspectives: according to function, by areas or topics, and from an institutional framework. In reality, institutional programs may contain an array of topical areas distributed according to several functions that educational planners have accepted as being historically and philosophically congruent with the institutional mission and objectives. As noted earlier each of these dimensions of programs is subject to pressures arising from larger and broader developments in the political, social, and economic life of a society.

Given the multiple meanings of the term when used to organize descriptive information concerning educational programs for adults and the sensitivity of the structural elements of each concept to social change, we may ask what we know about the planning processes themselves. These processes exist on three levels: the ideal, the real, and the procedures planners say they use. For our purposes we shall examine the ideal processes as they are derived from reported procedures. These procedures are noted because they usually reflect an awareness of change (through need-identification procedures) as a factor influencing educational programs.

PROGRAM-PLANNING PROCESSES

Program development as generally discussed in the literature of the field is concerned with certain procedures used by the specialist to give reality to an educational idea for a particular audience engaged in discrete adult education activities and/or programs. The process is thus initiated by an idea and is concluded by the terminal evaluation of a particular activity or program that is integrated into the larger institutional program. London (1960, p. 66) identifies five steps in program development. They are listed on page 18.

TABLE 1.2:   Sources of Education and Learning in the United States

DELIBERATE EDUCATION AND LEARNING		
	Usual Age of Students	*Approximate Number of Participants (in millions)*
I. Schools		
A. Preprimary education	1–4	10.0
B. Elementary & secondary education	5–17	42.0
C. College & university under- graduate education	18–21	9.5
D. Graduate & professional education	21–27	1.5
E. Public school adult education	16 and older	1.8
F. Proprietary schools	18 and older	1.2
G. University extension and continuing education	28 and older	3.3
H. Community education	All ages	.5
II. Nonschool organizations		
A. Private industry		5.8
B. Professional associations		5.5
C. Trade unions		.6
D. Government service		3.0
E. Federal manpower programs		1.7
F. Military services		1.5
G. Agriculture extension		12.0
H. City recreation departments		5.0
I. Community organizations		7.4
J. Churches and synagogues		3.3
K. Free universities		.2
L. Parks and forests	No meaningful estimate	
III. Individually used sources		
A. Personal—at hand	Virtually everyone	
B. Personal—at a distance	Virtually everyone	
C. Travel	Virtually everyone	
D. Print media	Virtually everyone	
E. Electronic media	Virtually everyone	
I. In the home	Virtually everyone	
II. Work	Virtually everyone	
III. From friends	Virtually everyone	
IV. Mass media	Virtually everyone	
V. Other sources (for example, travel, community activities, recreation, and entertainment)	Virtually everyone	

Note: From R. E. Peterson, K. P. Cross, J. R. Valley, S. A. Powell, T. W. Hartle, M. Kutner, & T. B. Hirabayashi, *Lifelong learning in America* (San Francisco: Jossey-Bass, 1979), pp. 15–16. Reprinted with permission.

1. Determine the needs of the constituents
2. Enlist their participation in planning
3. Formulate clear objectives
4. Design a program plan
5. Plan and carry out a system of evaluation

Bergevin, Morris, and Smith (1963, pp. 10–12) recommend a six-step procedure as follows:

1. Identify a common need or interest
2. Develop topics
3. Set goals
4. Select appropriate resources
5. Select appropriate techniques and subtechniques
6. Outline each activity and responsibility to be carried out

Boyle and Jahns (1970) propose a similar sequence of procedures based on a systematic consideration of (a) the situation to be changed or improved, (b) educational needs of the target group translated into appropriate educational objectives, (c) learning experiences and plans for their use according to the selected objectives, and (d) a design for evaluation.

More directly related to the topic under consideration here is a recent proposal of Schroeder (1980). He has contributed to an improved conceptualization of the linkage between educational programs and the broader society. Schroeder presents adult and continuing education as a developmental process that links two systems, the agent system and the learner system, to establish directions and procedures for educational programs. According to his construct, the process involves six major decision points, each of which is informed by variables in the agent and client systems involved. The variables interact with the decision points to form a developmental system. At the decision points, the planner is concerned with what will be done at the macrolevel and microlevel. Macrolevel decisions establish general directions and procedures; microlevel decisions are more specific and are referred to as instructional or learning decisions. Macrolevel decision points include educative needs and educational program objectives and procedures; microlevel decision points include learning needs, objectives, and experiences.

Schroeder's proposal helps us to examine the social change dimension of program development. Adult educators long have been implicitly encouraged to look at events occurring in the larger so-

ciety for program development ideas. None of the program development models examined here, however, explicitly addresses the act of
social analysis as a useful procedure in program development.
Schroeder's macrolevel decision point concerning educative needs
and the first step in the procedures of London (1960), Bergevin et
al. (1963), and Boyle and Jahns (1970) are implicitly related to the
idea of social analysis, but they fail to be adequately explicated in the
literature on program development.

A NEW MODEL

The failure of current models, with the exception of Schroeder's concept, to explicitly address the historical and broader social, psychological and technological variables in program planning is an important oversight. Therefore, the following pages provide a discussion
of four fundamental assumptions or premises that should guide the
program-planning and program development processes. The four assumptions provide the foundations for this volume; they are as follows:

1. Awareness of larger social issues, events, and trends can be
   instructive in the planning of adult and continuing education
   activities and programs.
2. Adult and continuing education activities and program planning are informed and rewarded by adherence to historical
   characteristics of the field such as dynamism, pluralism,
   pragmatism, and voluntarism.
3. Philosophical concerns such as the purpose of adult and continuing education and the people it should serve interact with
   variables in each of these assumptions.
4. Programming in adult and continuing education is creative.

Each of these assumptions is illustrated in figure 1.1. These assumptions do not obviate the need for specific location and audience-
planning strategies such as those suggested by Bergevin et al., Boyle
and Jahns, and others. Rather, the concept suggested here is similar
to Schroeder's provision for considering macrolevel variables. Consideration of both macrolevel and microlevel variables in program
planning will contribute to the success of the process.

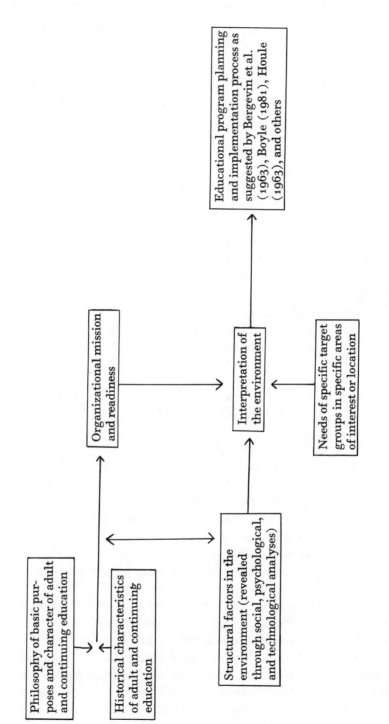

FIGURE 1.1: A Heuristic Educational Program-Planning Model Incorporating Historical and Macro Elements

AWARENESS OF SOCIAL ISSUES

An underlying premise of the model and this book is that knowledge of larger social issues, events, and trends can be instructive in the program development process. We should examine the implications of these social, psychological, and technological phenomena for the creation and delivery of adult education programs. It is sufficient to observe that the issues, events, and trends that are noteworthy in the national and regional framework often will need to be reviewed from the perspective of the local population served by a specific adult education institution. Thus, there is a macrolevel analysis and a microlevel analysis, to follow Schroeder's system.

The idea of interaction between adult and continuing education and the larger society is pursued in depth in an interesting and informative work published by the Council of Europe (1980). That work discusses the ways in which adult and continuing education in Europe is influenced by the social context in which it operates, but it is also noted that adult and continuing education should have some impact upon this context. It is suggested that individuals who seek to understand programming in adult and continuing education within the framework of the social context should begin from a socio-philosophical analysis. The fundamental sociological issue is the degree of independence the educational subsystem has of the broader society. The answer to this problem helps to inform the question of the role of education in society. For example, is education a factor in the "reproduction of society generation after generation or is it a factor for change? Or put another way, does education contain some factors of change and some factors of reproduction, more or less of each according to varying circumstances?" (Council of Europe, 1980).

Based on several years of analysis, the council notes a number of trends in the development of adult and continuing education in Europe. Some of these major trends are discussed briefly here because they are related to the basic concepts of this volume and because the results of the European analysis should prove beneficial to American program planners and administrators. Four dominant trends are discussed in the following paragraphs.

There is a trend toward globalization of the educational activity. Another term for *globalization* that may be more acceptable to

Americans is *holistic*. The concept implies considering the entire person within the total environment when planning educational programs. The idea is readily admitted to be an "ideal" that will continue to escape attainment; nevertheless, it provides a worthy goal for purposes of reflecting on the content and structure of the learning experience. Holistic education has two characteristics: It is not divorced from the process of daily living, and it provides the means of acting upon the environment.

The fundamental properties of the globalization concept are basic to the other three trends. The second trend represents performance in life as a primary objective of adult and continuing education. The third trend concerns the development of adult education from the "outward perspective." Aspects of this trend include the effects of access to education by those who have heretofore been poorly served. Other effects are noted in the planning processes that seek to require that adult education develop parallel to related economic and cultural developments. The fourth trend is concerned with development from the "inner perspective." It is consistent with the idea that adult education is changed so that the life it offers its students is more consonant with the life it tries to enable them to obtain in the world at large. The characteristics of this trend include involvement of the learners in the planning and execution of the educational activity and the recognition that life is a source of knowledge as well as the object of application of knowledge. Similar impacts of the trend are noted in other areas such as in effects on the knowledge base and on the methodology and the roles of adult educators (Council of Europe, 1980).

The study of the development of adult education in Europe also identifies some of the program areas that are discussed more fully in chapters 5–8. The independent development of the European study and this volume and the similarity of our conclusions provide additional support for our premises: (a) that adult and continuing education interacts with broader social events including economic, political, and technological changes, and (b) that consequently, program activity should be informed by an awareness of the implications of such events.

HISTORICAL CHARACTERISTICS

A second premise concerning programming in adult and continuing education concerns the underlying historical principles of the field. As noted earlier adult and continuing education programs in the United States have reflected certain inherent characteristics such as creativity, pragmatism, voluntarism, pluralism, and dynamism (Long, 1980b). Program planners in the eighteenth and nineteenth centuries, just as those of the twentieth century, were often rewarded when they recognized those five characteristics, and there is reason to believe that they were penalized when they failed to recognize them.

Analyses of current events—social, psychological, and technological—and any subsequent program ideas that are generated through the analyses should be examined against a historical background.

The relationship between broad social changes or events with pervasive cultural consequences and adult and continuing education has not been adequately or systematically studied. There are some examples, however, that seem to lend credence to the existence of a relationship. Titmus (1981) provides some convincing evidence through his analysis of adult and continuing education in Europe. The Danish folk school is a useful example. The expansion of evening schools in colonial America as discussed by Long (1976) also provides another good historical example. Both of these institutions developed out of specific social conditions; the folk school was a means to revive a nation's pride and the evening school emerged out of the unique economic and demographic characteristics of eighteenth-century America. There is some reason to speculate that the "nontraditional" concepts of education that spread throughout the United States in the 1960s and 1970s are a contemporary manifestation of the premise. Furthermore, some of the nontraditional concepts have been adopted by existing "traditional" institutions.

The evolvement of new and different institutions may be justified occasionally, but more often adult and continuing education personnel are concerned with less spectacular programming challenges. They are usually more concerned with the way social, psychological, and technological developments will influence new and old target audiences and subsequent administration of educational programs. For example, how did ideas of social justice and equity affect the readiness of women and blacks to participate in adult and continuing education? How did these ideas stimulate educational planners to develop minority education programs? How will changing attitudes toward, and of, aging Americans be reflected in educational programming? What is the relationship between leisure and participation in adult and continuing education? Is the acceptance of electronic media for educational purposes more likely under certain social psychological conditions than others? How will home computers and advances in satellite communication affect educational programming activity? While these questions are not to be answered here, it is our purpose to contribute to further thinking about, and awareness of, broad social, psychological, and technological change in terms of its impact on programming in adult and continuing education.

PHILOSOPHICAL CONCERNS

A third premise affecting program development is that educational programming is influenced by philosophical concerns such as the purpose of education and the availability of larger audiences. These concerns interact with variables included in the previously discussed assumptions. Bryson's classification of the functions of adult and continuing education (1936) illustrates one philosophical orientation.

CREATIVE PROGRAMMING

A fourth premise of the program-planning model is based on the suggestion that planners bring imagination, creativity, and originality to bear on a process that is also affected by their sensitivity to the history and objectives of adult and continuing education. The most successful planners of education for adults show high levels of sensitivity that are translated into innovative programs. It is not clear how this sensitivity is stimulated, but it is probably cued by an alertness to subtle shifts in attitudes, moods, opinions, and behavior. Such shifts are likely noted as a result of the continuing immersion of the planners in the content of selected social indicators. It is not magic, and it is not completely the wooing of the muse; rather, an analytical approach to selected variables such as those discussed in this book results in sound program ideas. As a consequence of the application of this fourth premise, the program planner is equipped to design, conduct, analyze, and interpret needs-assessment activities within specific target populations and geographic areas (communities, states, region, nation) and within selected target audiences (the aging, women, disadvantaged) concerning identified functions (remedial, occupational, relational, liberal and political education).

The concept explicated here does not replace specific location-, group-, or individually based needs-assessment procedures. Instead, it stimulates, supplements, and enriches specific needs-assessment activities by providing the educator/planner with a comprehensive background for investigation. Consequently, individual educational activities and programs are part of a larger universe and derive importance and relevance from broader social and historical relations.

As the twenty-first century looms close, adult educators are discovering even greater diversity in the possibilities for continuing education programs. Some of the developments are attributable to increasing sensitivity to the needs of special populations such as minority and ethnic groups, women, and individuals historically poorly served by educational institutions (as in the case of corrections education and educational opportunities for mentally and physically handicapped adults). Other new opportunities, such as adult and continuing education for the aged, are associated with broad social change. Still other possibilities are given impetus by a combination of changing concepts of social responsibility and technological change, as reflected in mandatory continuing education requirements in certain professional areas.

These rather general observations illustrate a historical phenomenon in adult and continuing education. The field continues to be dynamic and pluralistic when specific social, educational, and governmental institutions are considered. It has stubbornly resisted becoming a captive of any one philosophy, institution, or program area and continues to respond successfully to the continuing education needs of American adults. The dynamism and pluralism of adult and continuing education in America frequently challenge practitioners, theoreticians, and students of the field in their efforts to obtain an informed view of contemporary programmistic developments.

Several developments in recent years encourage a fresh analytical and descriptive overview of programmatic topics in adult and continuing education. Some of these developments, such as increased awareness of the educational needs of special populations, have already been alluded to. Two other developments include the changing demographic profile that is referred to as the "graying of America" and a concomitant increasing popular acceptance of lifelong learning. These and other changes will be more fully explicated later; it is sufficient to note here that their developments are significant and pervasive. Consequently, they have practical implications for professional adult and continuing educators in a host of institutional settings from the ubiquitous community college to business and industry. Thus, as noted at the beginning of this chapter, we can expect changes in concepts of education and learning to parallel other ideological, political, sociological, technological, and economic changes in society.

SUMMARY

Programs of adult and continuing education are directly and indirectly influenced by events and developments of a social, psychological, and technological nature. Program activities affected by such developments are of two kinds: content and process. While it is axiomatic to observe that a relationship exists between the larger society and the educational process, the interaction is not sufficiently explicit in the program literature of adult and continuing education.

This discussion has put forth the premise that programming in adult and continuing education should be informed by an awareness of the historical attributes of the field as well as by a sensitivity to social, psychological, and technological developments. These theoretical constructs have practical implications for the content of adult and continuing education programs. Furthermore, the model given here simultaneously provides for generally recognized program-planning procedures, such as identifying the purposes, needs, and objectives of adult education, appropriate resources (including delivery mechanisms and marketing activity), and evaluation concepts and practices.

PART II

Impetus
for Program Changes

Social, Psychological,
Technological, Educational,
and Administrative Developments

Overview

We have noted the interplay between educational programming for adults and new social structures, concepts
of the individual, and inventions that change the workplace, home, and leisure activities. Education influences
the social context, and society in turn affects educational
programming for adults. For example, educational activities contribute to modifications in political and economic
attitudes. Greater awareness, say, of economic inequities
or political injustice may in turn be reflected in social
changes in areas such as interpersonal relations, work
structures, taxation, and welfare programs. Subsequently,
structural and attitudinal changes in these areas are further reflected in educational needs and interests. Different
people may become the object of new programs and special institutions; different methods may emerge to meet
the newly recognized populations and educational needs.

As we saw in the introduction, the development of
sound and successful programs for adults is a complex
process. Some of the sources for program change are sub-
sumed in this volume under the broad headings of social,
psychological, technological, administrative, and educational developments.

It is obvious that the social, psychological, and technological all interact and that it is difficult to clearly distinguish a social development from a psychological or
technological one. This system of classification has been
adopted here, however, for purposes of convenience, and
the reader is encouraged to accept it without too much
quibbling.

Demographic trends, interest in education, attitudes
toward education, and declining academic abilities are
among the topics discussed as social developments in chapter 2. Some of the trends noted are in two streams that
seem to be flowing in different directions. Contradictory
developments in the broader society pose difficulties for
program planners; where trends are consistently unidirec-
tional and mutually supporting, then the program planner's job is much easier. Unfortunately, few such trends
are identifiable. An example of potentially conflicting
positions concerns the demographic profile of the nation.
On the one hand, participation of older Americans in
adult and continuing education activities is much lower
than the rate of participation of other adult age groups.
Conversely, educational achievement level, measured in
years of schooling, is one of the best predictors of adult
participation. By 1990 the American population will be
older, with a larger percentage of individuals above age
55. These individuals will also have a higher level of educational achievement than did members of this age group
in 1970. How these two variables will be affected by other
factors such as retirement and the general economy is
not known. Planners will be challenged to speculate about
the future if they are to maintain competitive positions
in the provision of adult and continuing education.

Similar observations can be made about the psychological and technological changes that have been noted. For example, there is now great support for the concept of lifelong learning. Ample evidence shows that older adults can learn efficiently and effectively. At the same time, we are experiencing an apparent decline in academic skills that will soon permeate the teaching force as well as the learning force. If the abilities of adult and continuing educators decline, how will that affect the provision of sound educational programs for adults? Topics of a psychological nature discussed in chapter 3 include the changing appreciation of the adult ability to learn, participation data, the popularity of self-directed learning, human values, hemispheric brain research, cognitive styles, and adult life stages.

The situation concerning technology is not clear either. Not only does technology include the hardware that constitutes many inventions such as robots, computers, and advances in electronic communications; it also includes new organizational approaches and societal structures. Chapter 4, however, is primarily designed to discuss the electronic media as they may be used in adult and continuing education. Technology represents a great unknown when applied to education. On the one hand, it is seen as the means by which many issues associated with quality, travel, costs, and so forth are to be resolved. On the other hand, it may be argued that technology will only exacerbate many of the problems already confronting the discipline.

Chapter 5 describes some of the developments in educational and administrative concepts that have implications for programming in adult and continuing education. The first part of the chapter examines the preparation of adult and continuing educators. The second part directs attention to developments in administration of adult and continuing education programs. Developments in both of these areas have twofold implications for the field. First, they reveal changes that must be addressed.

Second, they represent programming opportunities for
different educational institutions and agencies. The continuing education needs of educators of adults, for example, are widely recognized by an increasing number of
consulting firms and other organizations that offer conferences on such diverse topics as marketing, understanding the adult learner, and needs-assessment and
evaluation.

The reader is reminded to keep the major theme of
the book in mind as Part II is read. The historical characteristics of adult and continuing education—creativity,
dynamism, pluralism, pragmatism, and voluntarism—
should be recalled. Within this framework the interaction
of the significant events of a period with educational programs for adults becomes apparent. Not only does education contribute to change in society, but we are also constantly reminded that changes in society bring about and
contribute to changes in adult education activities and
structures. How shall the various events and discoveries
identified in the following section be translated into
educational programs for adults?

2   Social Developments

Even the casual observer is aware of numerous and profound changes that have occurred in American society within the past 20 years. It is apparent that many of the changes carry the seeds of program opportunities. A few changes gleaned from popular sources are as follows:

- Increasing numbers of households are headed by a single parent, often a working mother.
- There are more "hybrid" families—remarried adults with children of previous marriages.
- The proportion of college-educated Americans has increased.
- Many college graduates will have to take jobs for which an earlier generation would have been overqualified (Jones, 1980).

Additional social developments that will soon influence programming in adult and continuing education are discussed in this chapter. They are: (a) changing age profiles, (b) rising educational levels, (c) growing concern about equity and the rights of special populations, (d) changing attitudes toward work, (e) career change, (f) professional and occupational obsolescence, (g) mandatory continuing education, (h) increasing acceptance of nontraditional approaches to education, and (i) the expansion of education.

Chapter 1 outlined a program-planning model based on the thesis that a number of historical, philosophical, and contemporary variables affect the creation and implementation of programs of adult and continuing education. The creative planner can take one or more of the nine social developments we have listed and establish relationships with the historical characteristics of adult and con-

tinuing education described in chapter 1. Within the framework of
the educator's philosophy of the basic purposes and characteristics of
adult education, and dependent upon the institutional readiness, program formats and procedures emerge.

For example, the development labeled "changing age profiles" is
considered within the planning model based on the following structures: (a) adult and continuing education is voluntary and dynamic,
(b) it is offered to people for personal self-actualization, (c) the institution has the capability and readiness to offer instruction in the
area of adult life-stage development, (d) changing age profiles for
a specific audience are identified and examined with implications
noted, (e) the general social, cultural, and physical environment as
it relates to the previous four points is examined, (f) surveys of
client groups identified in step (e) are conducted to ascertain more
specific interests and needs associated with the topic, and (g) planning procedures are initiated.

It is not my intention to go through this planning process for
each of the nine social developments listed here or others discussed
in the following chapters. My purpose is to *identify* important developments and thereby suggest to the creative mind related events of
importance to the planner. A brief discussion of practical implications is available in each of the following three chapters. Some of the
identified developments, as well as those the reader may note in addition, have dual implications. One set of implications is related to
content of programs, and the other set addresses process in the program-planning activity.

SCENARIOS FOR THE FUTURE

One principle of adult and continuing education is that it seems to
grow more rapidly in times of change (Peers, 1958). Change in recent years has been accelerating so rapidly, and has become so profound and pervasive, that all aspects of life are being subjected to a
process of continuous transformation. It is now clear that people cannot cope with the overpowering fact of massive change by an un-
critical application of what has been learned in the past, nor can they
cope by resorting to a strategy of trial-and-error improvisation.
McClusky has noted, "Our only hope lies in the realization of the
fact that continuous change requires continuous education. This is

true of the individual, of the community and the society at large" (1974, p. 101).

In recognition of the close association between adult and continuing education and social change, the College Board conducted an extensive national forum designed to identify potential alternate futures in the United States. The result was published under the title *Alternative Scenarios of the American Future—1980–2000* (Glover, 1979). The procedure included multiple surveys in a delphi technique mode of over 1,500 decision makers, educators, and scholars who, by virtue of their organizational roles, expertise, and reputations, were perceived as being in a position to influence the future directions of adult learning in the United States.

Participants in the forum responded to each of 120 statements concerning societal trends by providing (a) a forecast of the direction and rate of change for the trend from 1980 to 2000, (b) an assessment of its impact on life in the United States from 1980 to 2000, and (c) comments. Because the document reporting the survey results is too lengthy to describe here, a few selected trends will illustrate the findings.

1. Education and training expenditures will increase as a percentage of the U.S. GNP. Half of the respondents predicted an increase, and 49 percent rated the impact as favorable. Based on projected future developments, educators foresaw a gradual increase in investment in education and training for adult learning; the national investment will be in the form of tax credits, and student financial aid, entitlements, and tuition subsidies. Furthermore, they believed that training programs in the professions and occupations that support national goals and manpower will receive higher priority than those in general education. Public spending will shift from public school to junior and community colleges and technical institutes. Other opinions associated with this prediction include the following: (a) business will extend on-the-job training programs for women, low-income minorities, and the unemployed; (b) universities will negotiate contracts with employers to provide professional leadership and cultural programs for management; and (c) employers will expand staff development, job training, and educational fringe benefits for employees.

   Dissenting respondents believed that reductions in government spending and taxes have a higher priority than increased spending for education and training. Accordingly, they predicted that support for higher education will decline. They warned that increased support for lifelong learning will not come about simply because adult learners demand it; it will occur only as a result of well-organized political advocacy as adult programs compete with more established priorities such as programs concerning energy, health, unemployment, and aging.

2. Investment in human capital through continuing education and training of employees will increase. Eighty-three percent of the respondents predicted the increase, and 85 percent indicated that the impact would be favorable. Furthermore, respondents suggested that employers will recognize the necessity of continuing education and training to accomplish the following goals: (a) develop new technology and increase worker creativity and productivity, (b) maintain worker morale, (c) keep the knowledge and skill of their work force current, (d) equalize employment opportunities for women, minorities, and the handicapped, and (e) fulfill collective bargaining contracts, which will build in education demands.

Dissenting survey participants argued that employers will place the burden of responsibility for upgrading job skills on individual employees. They believed that with inflation and higher taxes and wages, business will spend less rather than more on staff development and training. These respondents also thought that large corporations will invest heavily in leadership management while small businesses will not. Since most Americans work in small firms, the corporate investment is perceived as benefiting only a small percentage of workers.

3. Dependence of the public on professionals for knowledge and information required to satisfy human needs will increase. The impact of this development is uncertain according to the opinions of the respondents. Thirty-six percent indicated that the development would have a mixed impact, 33 percent predicted that the impact would be favorable, and 31 percent suggested that the impact would be unfavorable.

The respondents believed that recent criticism suggests a growing popular reaction against professional elites who have used their clients' dependence to promote their own self-interest. The educators therefore predicted the following developments:

(a) policymakers will expect professionals to justify their support and to be accountable for the quality of services, (b) well-educated clients will expect to participate on a more equal basis with professionals in decisions that affect their lives, and (c) adult education will sometimes conflict with the vested interest of professionals whose high levels of income result from client dependence. According to the respondents, in the future the public will demand that professionals help clients to solve their own problems. At the same time, the interest of professional practitioners will be threatened by educational programs that enable paraprofessionals and clients to function more independently.

Additional social changes that have educational implications are discussed in the following pages.

SELECTED CHANGES

CHANGING AGE PROFILES

Following the baby boom of the Second World War, American institutions seemed to reflect an assumption that the rising tide of young faces would be a permanent feature. By 1975, however, following a number of years of stable or reduced birth rates, demographers began predicting the "graying of America." The aging of the American population is pictured as a series of waves spaced ten years apart, to coincide with the U.S. Census; some of the waves are higher than others because the number of individuals in each ten-year period is different. As viewed from 1980, the "big" wave or bulge in the population data represents individuals 25 to 35 years of age. This wave will move across the future of America through the early part of the next century and will dominate the profile until it vanishes or a new larger one appears.

In the 1970s and 1980s, the young adults of the postwar baby boom thus became the consumers of adult and continuing education. Assuming that another principle of the field prevails, that "participants in adult education continue to participate," individuals in the cohort should participate at a higher level than have individuals in other cohorts at advanced ages.

The graying of America will influence numerous areas of life including employment, economics, politics, religion, family relationships, and education. Adjustment in each of these important areas will have an impact on the field of adult education.

Before looking at how some of these changes may affect adult educators, we should establish a common understanding of the projected demographic profile. In 1977, 51 percent of all Americans were under 30 years of age. By the year 2000, that group will represent only 42 percent of the population. Finally, by 2030 the under-30 group will total 40 percent of all Americans. The largest percentage of increase will occur within the group 65 years or older. In 1977 the older age group equaled 11 percent of the national population. By 2030, 18 percent of all Americans will be at least 65 years of age. This is a change from about one of ten to one of five Americans being 65 years old.

The increasing political muscle of the older American is already seen in national legislation. Changing attitudes and legislation concerning mandatory retirement did not occur in a vacuum. Similar modifications to Social Security legislation that resulted in increased payments by younger individuals and by employers indicate that some politicians have been sensitized to the changing age mix. Perhaps the real test of the political strength of older Americans will concern future Social Security benefits. At this writing the Reagan administration has been testing the situation to see how much the Social Security system can be modified. It is instructive to observe that changes to date have been primarily limited to benefits that do not affect the total population of recipients.

Politicians are not the only ones who will feel the impact of change. Educators may discover new needs and reject some traditional concepts. Emerging program areas that are already posing problems and holding promise include the array of counseling services and career education concepts. Adult educators also seem to be caught between the increasing trend toward renewable certificates and/or relicensure requirements that may require certification of competencies and the philosophical principle that opposes "testing" the adult learner.

The aging of America will likely have an impact on the development and acceptance of lifelong learning as a formal philosophical concept. Lifelong learning now enjoys a rather informal status, but it is likely to be more commonly accepted because the percentage of

individuals in the age group currently served by continuing education programs will peak in the year 2000. It is estimated that just 20
years from now, 45.5 percent of all Americans will be 30 to 64 years
of age.

The older adult in the year 2000 will be a very different older
person in terms of educational attainment, nutrition and health
status, material resources, expectations, and years of useful life remaining. The gerontological descriptions of two categories, the
"young old," aged 65 to 75, and the "old old," over the age of 75,
will become even more useful. The young old constitute about two-
thirds of the total over-65 age group, and they generally possess few
of the negative health or personal characteristics that are popularly
associated with old age. Persons in this age group are relatively
healthy, mobile, prosperous, alert, and active. Many of the young
old have little or no need for supportive services; furthermore, they
are living life with considerable satisfaction. One of the few things
that differentiates the young old from persons aged 55 to 64 is that
many of them have additional leisure as a consequence of retirement.

While there may be some questions about how the aging trend
may affect occupational mobility, there is little doubt that it will encourage the development of employment-related continuing education. The aging of America and the move away from mandatory retirement present interesting opportunities for alternative scenarios.
One scenario suggests that older adults will strive to hold career posi-
ions while efforts will be made by younger employees or even the
unemployed to challenge them for their jobs. Such a scenario suggests that adults of all ages may be competing to maintain relative
skills and develop new competencies as technology and social change
requires.

Almost every scenario of the future based on the demographic
predictions reported here must include adult and continuing education as a critical element. Adults will likely use educational opportunities in differing ways than they now do. Continuing education related to the world of work will reflect different motives and goals.
For example, the prospect of greater employee loyalty may encour-
.age the development of a continuing education curriculum as opposed to the cafeteria approach. Stresses in the political system may
even stimulate an increased awareness of the potential of adult education in public affairs.

At present adult educators are at one of those important crossroads that may have long-term impact on individual programs. They are challenged to determine how the new age mix in society will affect the programming strategies that have evolved during a youth-oriented decade. Failure to be alert and sensitive to the aging of America will deleteriously affect the future of adult and continuing education.

RISING EDUCATIONAL LEVELS

Each decade since 1900, the national average educational achievement level has increased. The general diffusion of educational opportunity has been a factor in American society for over one hundred years, and the trend is likely to continue. It is safe to predict an expanding clientele for adult learning activities because the kinds of people who participate in continuing education are becoming an increasingly larger proportion of our adult population.

The literature on participation in these programs consistently agrees on two points: Persons who have a high level of educational achievement are more likely to take part in adult and continuing education than those who have fewer years of education, and the aging population is characterized by rising educational achievement levels (Johnstone & Rivera, 1965; Morstain & Smart, 1974; Saindon, 1982). The parallel social developments include the rising educational level of the current young and middle-aged adults and the increasing proportion (and absolute numbers) of middle-aged and older adults projected for the year 2000 (see table 2.1 for a compari-

TABLE 2.1:   Participation in Adult Education by Educational Attainment

	1969		1975		1978	
	Partici- *pation*	*Total* *Adult Pop.*	*Partici-* *pation*	*Total* *Adult Pop.*	*Partici-* *pation*	*Total* *Adult Pop.*
Less than high school	15.2%	44.6%	10.3%	36.5%	9.9%	33.8%
High school	38.8%	35.9%	37.5%	36.6%	33.5%	36.8%
More than high school	46.0%	19.5%	52.2%	26.9%	56.7%	29.5%

Source: National Center for Education Statistics, *The condition of education* (Washington, D.C.: U.S. Government Printing Office, 1980).

son of participation for three levels of educational achievement).
Riley and Foner (1968) indicate the age cohort that will be from 65
to 69 in the year 2000 will have an average of 12.3 years of education (males and females) while the group that was from 65 to 69 in
1976 had only a median number of 9.4 (for males) and 10.1 (for females) years of education. In 1976, 7.6 percent of those aged 65 to
69 were functionally illiterate, having fewer than four years of
schooling, compared with 10.4 percent for those in the age group 70
to 74, 13.3 percent for those 75 to 79, and 18.2 percent for persons
80 and older. In contrast, it is predicted that in the year 2000, only
2.9 percent of persons over 65 will have had fewer than four years
of formal education. The same trend can be seen for the immediate
future. The percentage of persons over 65 who have not completed
eight years of school will have dropped from 60.6 percent to 39.0
percent by 1985. At the same date, the proportion of those 65 and
over who have completed one or more years of college will have
shown a 5-percent increase, from 11 to 16 percent.

Changes in attitude are as important as demographic changes.
The present group of elderly persons has what some would consider
a disappointing rate of participation in educational activities. In 1972
only 2.4 percent of persons over 65 were enrolled in adult educational programs, and only 6.3 percent of the age group 55 to 64 had
participated in adult education programs during the prior year
(Academy for Educational Development, 1974). Reasons for this low
level of participation include cost, inconvenience, transportation
problems, attitudes toward self and toward educational institutions,
and anxiety over negative attitudes on the part of faculty and other
students. The fact is that the current generation of older adults has
not been served well by traditional educational institutions, many of
which remain oriented exclusively toward youth. More is said concerning this topic in chapter 3.

CONCERN FOR SPECIAL POPULATIONS

All participation studies indicate that the most favored segments
of the population are the most frequent consumers of adult and continuing education. The least favored, including minorities, ethnic
groups, and other special populations such as the handicapped, do
not participate as often.

The seventh and eighth decades of the twentieth century were times of momentous social ferment. Previously held attitudes and values were frequently questioned, and a new sensitivity toward special populations emerged. Perhaps the vanguard of the new philosophy was concern for the economically and educationally disadvantaged as represented by the millions of illiterate adults in the United States. This concern was expanded to include ethnic groups, new immigrants, the elderly, inmates in correctional institutions, and clients in mental hospitals. Even though Johnstone and Rivera's (1965) survey found no sex differences in participation, women were included in this population as a group perceived to have been previously unjustly served by social and legal agencies.

Out of the new sensitivity for the special populations, a number of new programmatic challenges developed. For example, how could planners reach the previously undereducated and serve their needs? Numerous studies have been conducted to describe ways of recruiting the unlettered for learning, and an equal mass of investigation has been concerned with how to keep them enrolled once they have enlisted for education. The intensity of the problem is well summarized by Valley (Peterson et al., 1979), who notes that 90 percent of the participants in adult learning are high school graduates with 30 percent being college graduates.

As the average participant in adult and continuing education is Caucasian, relatively affluent, well educated, and employed, the inverse of the generalization defines the consequences of policies that fail to provide for equity. Minorities and the socially disadvantaged are not participating in adult and continuing education in proportion to their numbers of the eligible adult populations. Moreover, it appears that their rate of participation is declining. The success differential between special continuing education programs for women, for example, and other populations discussed in this section illustrates how certain social and economic factors interact in the different populations.

The trend conflicts with the federal policy for education that appears to have been most clearly articulated and most universally accepted, that of equal access and equal opportunity. This is an important objective that remains to be achieved in adult and continuing education. There is reason to believe that while the distance between educational supply and demand has been reduced for many members of the special populations, for many individuals, that distance has probably been increased. See tables 2.2 and 2.3 for information on participation by race and income.

CHANGING ATTITUDES TOWARD WORK

Like many of the other important implications of social changes discussed thus far, the probable effects of changing American attitudes toward work upon adult and continuing education are difficult to identify. While social scientists have debated the association between the Protestant ethic and the genesis of capitalism, they generally agree that thrift, hard work, and a capacity for deferring gratification historically were traits widely distributed among Amer-

TABLE 2.2:   Participation in Adult Education by Race

	1969		1972		1975	
	Partici- pation	Total Adult Pop.	Partici- pation	Total Adult Pop.	Partici- pation	Total Adult Pop.
White	91.5%	89.3%	92.3%	89.0%	92.3%	88.4%
Black	7.5%	9.7%	6.4%	9.9%	6.0%	10.1%
Other	1.0%	1.0%	1.3%	1.1%	1.7%	1.5%

Source: National Center for Education Statistics, *The condition of education* (Washington, D.C.: U.S. Government Printing Office, 1980).

TABLE 2.3:   Participation in Adult Education by Income

	1969		1975		1978	
	Partici- pation	Total Adult Pop.	Partici- pation	Total Adult Pop.	Partici- pation	Total Adult Pop.
Less than $10,000	45.5%	59.1%	25.3%	37.3%	34.4%	48.0%
More than $10,000	54.6%	40.9%	70.5%	54.7%	61.1%	43.9%
Not reported	0.0	0.0	4.2%	8.0%	4.5%	8.1%

Source: National Center for Education Statistics, *The condition of education* (Washington, D.C.: U.S. Government Printing Office, 1980).

icans. Furthermore, according to the argument that legitimates the economic system, individuals are assumed to be responsible for their own circumstances. These opinions or social values appear to be under attack. To illustrate this point, some futurists tell us that automation will make work unnecessary for many people, and that the emphasis on work should be decreased in favor of other life-style elements such as leisure. In the publication *Work in America* (Upjohn Institute, n.d.), attention is drawn to the following alleged signs of the obsolescence of work: (a) the growth in the number of communes, (b) the presence of numerous adolescents panhandling in such meccas as Georgetown in Washington, D.C., and North Beach and the Sunset Strip in California, (c) a shift to the four-day work week by various enterprises, (d) a growth in welfare case loads, and (e) increasingly earlier retirement. All of these are relatively benign signs, but more malignant signs are found in the reduction of productivity, the increase in man days per year lost from work through strikes, and a rise in absenteeism, industrial sabotage, and turnover rates.

Two recently completed studies appear to confirm a relationship between workplace satisfaction and participation in educational activities. Saindon's (1982) research reveals that work-related opportunities to develop abilities are a useful predictor of participation in vocational training but not participation in general education. A study of Canadian health professionals generated similar results: Quastel and Boshier (1982) indicate that job dissatisfaction is associated with the absence of opportunities to satisfy needs for learning. Thus, developments that affect the workplace also have a way of reaching into educational structures in a number of ways.

Career change is one of the social developments related to work that has received considerable attention in recent years. This body of literature emphasizes the decisions of men and women to move from one chosen area of work to another.

Career Change

Since the publication of Sheehy's (1976) best seller *Passages: Predictable Crises of Adult Life,* the concept of mid-life career change has been one of the more popular topics in adult and continuing education. Sheehy drew heavily from the work of Daniel

Levinson, whose basic thesis is that the life structure evolves through a standard sequence of periods. The periods and eras of which they are a part are a basic underlying source of order in the life cycle (Levinson et al., 1978). Levinson divides adulthood into three stages: (a) early adulthood, lasting from 17 to 40, (b) middle adulthood, from 40 to 60, and (c) late adulthood, from age 60 onward. Theoretically, each of the adult life stages, particularly the first two, contains discrete evolutionary points at which adults enter for development, accustom themselves to their situation, and then settle down to its benefits and challenges. Furthermore, it is suggested that each clear development stage is preceded by an unsettling transition period (Levinson et al., 1978).

Adult educators are particularly concerned about the implications of life-stage development for career change and related educational needs. Unfortunately, little has been written on the subject from the perspective of the adult and continuing educator. Arbeiter (1979) provides an extremely logical and cogent discussion of mid-career life transition. His work, however, would have been even more valuable had he had the opportunity to more directly address each of the three life stages posited by Levinson.

Occupational Change, Career Change, and Geographical Mobility. It is evident that adult education participation patterns vary across the life-span according to age and other variables such as educational achievement, income, and occupation. It is also clear that occupational, geographical, and career mobility in America are all high, and that they are in some way related to participation in adult education.

Census data over recent decades confirm the truism that American society is mobile. Geographic mobility is easily defined as a move from one residence to another. Its impact is often mitigated by the local nature of the address change, for approximately one-half of all movers move within the same county. Career and occupational mobility are not frequently distinguished; subsequently, discussion on this point is sometimes confusing. The tendency of Americans to change employment is as well known as is their proclivity to change addresses. However, what does a change in employment actually mean? When does an employment change constitute a career change?

Employment or *occupational change* is an inclusive term that can include a change from one major job classification to another. Such a change could be within or between the 12 major employment groups or from one to another of 417 job categories or from one employer to another. It is obvious that a change from one employer to another is a minimal change; for example, a service station attendant might move from one station to another. The difference between the first two kinds of employment changes, however, is not always clear. Arbeiter (1979) is persuasive in his argument that many changes within or between the 12 major employment group classifications, such as a move from an administrative position in higher education to a similar position in a public school system, do not constitute *career changes*. In contrast, he believes that a change from one to another of the 417 occupational categories included in the *Alphabetical Index of Industries and Occupations*, published by the Bureau of the Census (U.S. Department of Commerce, 1971), is more likely to constitute a career change; for example, a meter reader changes jobs to become a photographer.

The distinction between a career change and an employment change helps providers of education to identify the age cohorts most likely to be involved in the respective changes. Furthermore, the educational needs related to occupational change are perceived to differ from the educational needs involved in career change. There may be no real need for adult education to facilitate an employment change. In contrast, for some career changes, as from short-order cook to accountant, from lawyer to minister, and so forth, the need for adult and continuing education may be extensive.

What age groups are associated with occupational or career change? People younger than 40 are most visible in both occupational and career change. Career mobility is less than occupational mobility and has been rather stable over the past two decades (Arbeiter, 1979). Byrne (1975) reports career mobility to be about 8.7 percent per year. Furthermore, the concept of mid-life career change notwithstanding, Byrne reports that the rate of career mobility declines steadily from the high point of 37.3 percent registered by men aged 18 to 19 to the 3.3 percent noted among men aged 45 to 54. The data for women are generally parallel to those for males except there is an aberration in the trend data for women 65 and over. This oldest female group reports an increase over the next-to-oldest group (55 to 64).

These data and the foregoing discussion indicate that educators should reexamine their positions and clarify the associations between occupational change, career change, geographical mobility, and educational needs. The profile of the age group most active in adult education, those younger than 40, reveals higher rates of geographical, career, and occupational change at the youngest ages, 18 to 20, and lower rates at the upper ages, 35 to 40. After age 40 the trend is one of stability. Thus, whereas occupational and career change may be a great incentive for participating in continuing education among those 18 to 25, the contingencies of participation for those aged 40 to 45 may be quite different. Other concepts of career other than workplace or job tasks become organizing and structuring properties for those in the age group 40 to 60.

The rate and extent of social change mentioned earlier also present additional challenges for career development. Not all workers desire to make mid-life career changes; some wish to remain in familiar surroundings doing the same kinds of things. Unfortunately, even workers who desire stability are finding the possibility of achieving it to be decreasing. The code word in this area of change is *obsolescence*.

PROFESSIONAL AND OCCUPATIONAL OBSOLESCENCE

It can be observed that the industrial state really has little use for the worker who has been made obsolete by technological advancement. The former workers represent a political and social challenge that may be increasingly turned over to educational institutions. Even though this aspect of worker obsolescence is important and will possibly become more so with the increasing use of robots, continuing and adult educators have generally discussed obsolescence as it applies to the professional areas.

Most of the concern for occupational obsolescence has been in selected fields, frequently described as being on the cutting edge of knowledge. These high-level fields include the professions and management with particular emphasis on engineering, science, medicine, business management, and public administration. Employees in other areas in which the application of knowledge and new technology is central are also affected by the phenomenon.

Recent literature of adult and continuing education supports the position that occupational education for the professional and the blue collar worker is a primary challenge. The periodic requirements for workers in many fields to upgrade their knowledge is evident. As jobs change, there is a need to change occupational educational approaches to provide for periodic formal updating of knowledge. Faure nails the point home by observing that "the transition from the idea of initial training to that of continual education is the mark of modern pedagogy" (1972, p. 117).

The concern for obsolescence among professionals may prove to be an unfortunate preoccupation because it has diverted attention from problems of obsolescence in other sectors of the economy. For example, there is increasing evidence that the layoffs and growing unemployment noted in 1982 contributed to more generalized mental health problems among workers. Despite unemployment compensation and other social provisions to ease the impact of unemployment, the chronically unemployed are threatened at very basic psychological levels. Nevertheless, the concern has been with the professional to such an extent that a new term has entered our vocabulary: *mandatory continuing education.*

Mandatory Continuing Education

The adoption by many professional and trade associations of relicensure or recertification requirements is known as mandatory continuing education (MCE). The general acceptance of MCE for professionals is best explained by the convergence of a number of social forces during the 1970s. The general public was sensitized to the consequences of change in certain professional areas such as health care. At the same time, a consumer-oriented movement gained strength, and professional incompetence soon became an object of concern among political leaders and others influenced by special interests. Consequently, MCE addressed the goals of a number of different interest groups: consumers, educators, and some professional associations.

It is likely that originally the licensing of selected occupations and professions was perceived by the practitioner as a safeguard; today the concept has been broadened to suggest that not only do professionals deserve some kind of security, as provided by entry qualifications, but the public also deserves protection against the erosive influence of time, changes in knowledge, and new technology on practice. Hence, there are today myriad state laws requiring relicensure or recertification for individuals in countless occupations. For years the general public has been aware of the recertification requirement imposed on public-school teachers, but a number of other occupations have similar requirements. In many instances state laws give certain trade or professional associations such as the bar, nurses' associations, and medical associations the authority to establish continuing education criteria that are in turn recognized by the legal agency of the state.

The adoption by many professional and trade associations of relicensure or recertification requirements has not been universally accepted. Several prominent academic adult educators have expressed concern about MCE in its various forms. Some critics suggest that through relicensure requirements, the state is doing the work that should be done by associations, if at all.

The trend is so far advanced and so pervasive, however, that opponents of MCE will probably fail to generate sufficient muscle to redirect the movement. While the concept of MCE may be philosophically unpalatable to some, the idea that the public requires protection in critical areas seems to be subscribed to by many. Furthermore, there are other philosophical and pragmatic reasons why the associations and providers of adult and continuing education support MCE. Philosophically, support emerges from a favorable disposition toward education generally. Pragmatically, MCE may guarantee additional adult participants in educational programs.

Three procedures have been suggested to resolve the conflict between the rights of the professional and the rights of the consuming public. They are: (a) legally or professionally mandated formal continuing education, (b) periodic evaluation of competence, based on examination, observed performance, or other measurements, and (c) self-directed study, based on the professional's sense of responsibility, to assure that knowledge and competence are maintained (Frandson, 1980). According to Frandson, the three proposed solutions emphasize two important issues: the validity of the selected approach for accomplishing the goals and the rights of all parties concerned.

It is not the objective of this discussion to argue the pros and cons of the issues surrounding MCE; rather, we are concerned with the impact of the trend on programming in adult education. Naturally, the programming characteristics will be influenced by the de-

gree to which the issue is resolved and the popularity of the selected
approach.

ACCEPTING NONTRADITIONAL APPROACHES

After World War II, education increasingly became an instrument that had several functions: It "certified" an individual's eligibility for certain kinds of employment; it was accepted as a status
symbol; and it frequently became a way of certifying a person's
worth. Given these kinds of inducements, access to diplomas, certificates, and degrees increased in importance among adults. At the
same time, social forces such as geographical and occupational mobility militated against traditional approaches to college degree work.
The success of the urban university night school was translated into
other new approaches to schedules, curriculum, evaluation, and degree requirements. Thus, one characteristic of contemporary views
of adult and continuing education is an increasing acceptance of nontraditional approaches for certifying competence or merit. Many
Americans are interested in continuing education units (CEUs), certification of experience, credit by examination, and other combinations of self-directed learning activities. Interest in the nontraditional
approaches seems to be closely related to the growth of institutionally based adult and continuing education since about 1950. Individuals formerly denied access to higher education because of work
schedules, life-styles, and other factors have responded to alternative
procedures for identifying and certifying competence and knowledge.
    Tough's research (1971, 1978) concerning the self-directed
learning activities of adults stimulated numerous additional investigations. The studies agree that approximately 90 percent of all adults
annually engage in some kind of learning activity. These data have
generally been used to confirm that adults do not limit their learning
to enrollment in institutionally planned and delivered educational
activities.
    The combination of increasing social acceptance of nontradi-
tional approaches with the data base developed by investigations of
self-directed learning projects presents a number of implications for
adult and continuing education. More is said about some of the current nontraditional approaches in chapter 8.

EXPANSION OF EDUCATION

Since the mid-nineteenth century, when property taxes began to become a common means for financing public education, American education has become increasingly democratic. By the mid-twentieth century, a high school education was possible for most young men and women, even though a sizable proportion failed to take advantage of the opportunity. Soon after World War II, a college education was perceived as an attainable goal by many middle-class Americans, and many people from lower socioeconomic strata were encouraged to seek college educations.

In the 1950s and 1960s, hundreds of new community colleges were established throughout the land. The two-year schools were frequently described as open-door institutions that presented educational opportunities to adults of all economic conditions from all walks of life. California led the nation into the new era of community colleges with their multifunctional mission of college-parallel instruction, vocational-occupational education, and community services including adult education and human development. Other states such as Texas, Florida, Virginia, and North Carolina soon followed California's lead. Many states developed plans to build community colleges within commuting distance of 90 percent of the eligible population.

The development of the community college and the maturing of the institution over the last 30 years would not have been possible without the new valuation of education as an end in itself as well as a means for economic mobility. The same deep appreciation for education that supported the development of the community college also contributed to the enhancement of other postsecondary institutions from technical schools to large multipurpose universities.

During the past 30 years, many universities in addition to the traditional land grant universities began to recognize the importance of outreach programs such as assistance to business, industry, mines, and communities. General extension services were frequently enlarged during these years, and a new unit was added to the campus: the residential conference center.

Greatly influenced by the leadership of the W. K. Kellogg Foundation, schools across the nation developed residential facilities for short-term conferences lasting from one day to three weeks. Kellogg

Foundation grants were instrumental in establishing attractive residential centers at Michigan State, Notre Dame, Columbia, California Polytechnic, and the Universities of Chicago, Nebraska, Oklahoma, Georgia, and New Hampshire. The University of Minnesota, Wayne State, Ohio State, Pennsylvania State, the University of Maryland, and Appalachian State University are among the schools that built centers without Kellogg aid. These facilities contributed immensely to the evolution of more or less common approaches to conference program development and management.

The important developments in education discussed in this section should not be viewed as independent events. They constitute a gestalt of development based on common values, generally shared expectations, and similar aspirations held by adults from the Georgia peanut farmer to the Kansas wheat farmer to the Pacific fisherman to New York bankers and Chicago attorneys.

SUMMARY AND CONCLUSIONS

The events and trends discussed here clearly reveal that America has experienced significant social change in the past 20 years, much of it associated with demographic and economic developments. The young adult population—the cohort born between 1945 and 1960—is quite different from the 1930–1945 cohort, and a number of social changes are associated with the phenomenon.

The 1930–1945 cohort influenced the development of adult and continuing education programs during the 1960s and 1970s. This group brought its own values and aspirations and expectations into conference rooms, training sessions, and other educational settings. The impact of this cohort, however, seems to be reaching a stage where it will be moderated by that of the next age group.

Other developments discussed include rising educational levels throughout American society, greater interest in the rights of special populations, shifting attitudes toward work, increasing frequency of career and occupational change, occupational obsolescence, mandatory continuing education, increasing acceptance of nontraditional approaches to education, and finally, changing expectations and expansion of education.

IMPLICATIONS

The social developments reviewed in this chapter are generally encouraging for administrators and planners of adult and continuing education programs. Yet, they are highly general developments and require the program planner to structure ideas at a more specific level. For example, the planner must often consider a specific industry such as the automotive industry or an occupation such as secretarial work within the framework of obsolescence created by automation processes.

Social changes as broad and pervasive as those discussed in this chapter have multidimensional implications at both the macrolevel and microlevel of program development. Social developments frequently suggest certain kinds of content while parallel changes in other areas such as psychology and technology have less conspicuous implications for needs-assessment, delivery, resources, and evaluation. Furthermore, it is obvious that many of the social developments identified here are not independent of the psychological and technological developments discussed in other chapters. The same advances in electronic engineering that may result in occupational obsolescence also contribute to new ways of designing and delivering educational programs for adults.

As the social canvas with which program artists work is broad, it is easy to see the wisdom of limiting a discussion of implications of social developments to general concepts. Specificity of program structure is influenced by the planners' consideration of broad social developments within parameters dictated, or strongly suggested, by institutional mission, philosophy, and resources. Two illustrative social phenomena are the so-called narcissism of the young adult generation and occupational changes.

The range of social change discussed in this chapter may have an impact on the different phases of program development such as needs, objectives, resources, and philosophy. For example, assuming the description of the me generation has elements of truth, educators of adults must consider the needs and interests of individuals of that particular generation simultaneously with the needs of the broader society. For example, in a democratic society, there may be significant dangers associated with an overemphasis on the individual. Tension between the needs of the individual and those of society has always been part of adult education in the United States. The situation presented by the current young adult generation, however, differs somewhat from both the social context of nineteenth-century utopian literature and that of the twentieth-century reformers who promoted education for social action.

One available approach is to exploit the so-called narcissism of the young adult generation. Such exploitation would focus on self-improvement and human potential concepts with little concern for social implications. Programs consistent with this approach would include such content as health, recreation, ways of improving one's personal attractiveness, fashion, investment plans, use of leisure, and self-awareness/self-mastery. A different philosophical approach would identify "issues" that acute narcissism raises for a democratic society and develop programs designed to mitigate its deleterious effects on the broader society.

Several of the social changes discussed in this chapter are related to changes in occupations and income-producing activities. Aslanian and Brickell's study (1980) of transitions and participation in adult and continuing education and also the work of Saindon (1982) and others demonstrate the close relationship between the world of work and education. Changes in the workplace are frequently multidimensional: They precede as well as follow educational programming. It has been suggested, for example, that organizational changes follow hardware and software developments. Thus, educational programmers may examine possibilities in the areas of hardware change, software development, and organizational change. What fields are being changed by rapid hardware innovations? Who are the clients for programs in these areas? What are the resources available? and so forth. Engineering and electronics information specialists and managers are examples of individuals whose work is associated with specific kinds of hardware developments. Many of these same individuals are also concerned about software. In turn an even larger array of managers, supervisors, and employees are involved in organizational changes that reflect innovative production, delivery, and service adjustments. Thus, a variety of program possibilities are suggested by occupational changes. Prospects of participation in these activities are enhanced by related changes such as mandatory continuing education and nontraditional programming.

3 Psychological Developments

A number of psychological developments occurring in the last 20 years have affected adult and continuing education. Some examples are as follows:

- Acceptance of countercultural values by both the blue-collar class and the upper middle class has increased (Jones, 1980).
- Personal aspirations, self-confidence, and sophistication have risen (Jones, 1980).
- Women now aspire to both career and family (Jones, 1980).
- There is ambivalence between optimism and pessimism (Jones, 1980; Watts, 1981).
- Altruism is yielding to narcissism (Jones, 1980; Marin, 1975).
- People show low motivation and little appreciation for sacrifice and commitment (Jones, 1980).
- Awareness of a "new" consciousness is evident (Ferguson, 1980).
- Efforts are being made to coordinate right-brain–left-brain functions (Ferguson, 1980).
- Change has become acceptable to most Americans (Watts, 1981).

American attitudes, values, beliefs, and behaviors have been modified on a number of fronts. Protest and civil disobedience became rooted in the American way of life in the 1960s and flowered in a wide range of arenas from anti–Vietnam War activities to antinuclear and proenvironmental movements. The *moral majority* emerged as a term to identify people who have consolidated around issues such as opposition to abortion and legal gambling and support of prayer in the public schools. Religion and religious leaders receive increasing attention from the media. These are some of the kinds of changes identified here as psychological.

Some of the items discussed in this chapter as psychological developments are so intricately interwoven with social events that it is difficult to determine which caused which. For example, in chapter 2 we alluded to the increasing popularity of nontraditional educational arrangements. While the movement toward such arrangements came out of a particular social situation, it is obvious that the emergence of the idea was closely related to favorable attitudes and psychic needs that existed at the time. Other developments that may be labeled philosophical are also part of the interaction between the psychological and social. Most of our efforts to separate the social from the psychological or the philosophical are rather arbitrary. Nevertheless, we must do so in the interest of simplicity.

Psychological developments that have implications for programming in adult and continuing education are of at least two kinds. They are discussed in two divisions of the chapter. The first division is concerned with a new mind-set or general way of thinking. The second part deals with conceptualizations about how humans think, remember, learn, and behave.

A NEW MIND-SET

There seems to be little argument that psychologically the current generation of young adults (ages 18–40) differs from older generations. A number of explanations have been suggested. It is obvious that individuals born after 1945 have experienced life-styles distinct from those of individuals born before 1945. The younger generation has been referred to as the instant gratification generation. At the same time, it is the only cohort to live its entire life under multiple threats of atomic warfare, international boycotts, and environmental stress. DDT, acid rain, radioactive waste, and mammoth oil spills by supertankers may have replaced measles, polio, and smallpox as important concerns and health hazards.

The large group of young adults who began taking their place in society around 1965 has also been defined as the "me generation." Just as the generation contributed to the expansion of the baby foods and toy industries at an earlier date, it provided the mass for the human potential movement of the 1970s. Response from the me generation to the varied forms of human transcendence led one writer to react strongly to what he calls the "new narcissism" (Marin, 1975). He explains the embrace given to the human potential movement that focuses so exclusively on self as one way of ignoring one's larger moral responsibilities.

Others, such as Ferguson (1980), maintain that the human potential movement encourages identification with the needs of others. Satow (1979) does not take issue with Marin's description of the current young adult generation, but she chooses to debate two valid points with him. She argues that narcissism is incorrectly used as a psychoanalytic term to explain a cultural problem. Furthermore, she says that narcissism is depicted as a value-laden term to emphasize individual blame whereas she contends that the problem has institutional sources. Satow's argument that we cannot change ourselves independently of the institutions within which we develop, however, is contrary to the emphasis on personal responsibility of the human potential movement.

It is important to observe that "personal" responsibility, as used here, is distinct from the concept of civic or social responsibility. In the human potential movement, according to Marin, *personal responsibility* is a term that is used to indicate one's obligations to "self" as opposed to others. In this framework individuals are all-powerful and totally determine their own fates. They should not, therefore, feel guilt or shame about anyone else's fate; those who are poor and hungry must be so because they wished it upon themselves. Thus, the new narcissism places emphasis on the independent/responsible self while the older positions emphasized the *relationship* of self with others. However, a word of caution is desired here. Not all adherents of the human potential movement are as narcissistic as Marin indicates. It is possible to be humanistic and humane without the selfish ego-centered emphasis Marin has found in so many of his contacts with humanistically oriented psychologists and others (Ferguson, 1980).

Regardless of one's position on the new humanism that empha-

sizes personal rights, self-assertiveness, personal responsibility, and
ego satisfaction, it is evident that adult and continuing educators are
already challenged by a new mind-set. A number of other psychologically oriented changes also have potential significance for program development in adult and continuing education. Three additional developments to be discussed in the following pages are: (a)
broader acceptance of third force psychology, (b) growing cogni-
zance of differentiations between adult life phases with consequent
concern for concepts of adult development, and (c) increasing awareness that learning is a lifelong activity.

THE THIRD FORCE

The term *third force* is often used to distinguish psychologists who
place a heavier emphasis on humanistic concepts than do their be-
haviorally and cognitively oriented colleagues. Despite one's opinions about the negative and positive aspects of the human potential
movement, it is clear that the 1980s have witnessed an increasing
sensitivity to the "human" aspects of the adult learner. Furthermore,
educators of adults seem to be especially attracted to the humanistic
theories of Abraham Maslow and Carl Rogers. The voluntary and
dynamic dimensions of adult and continuing education may well explain the awareness of human values that adult educators manifest.

The view of mankind based in part on the work of Rogers, Maslow, Carl Jung, and Gordon Allport presents the individual in positive human terms. The individual learner is frequently described as
a "self-actualizing," "becoming" person who is sufficiently motivated
to overcome many of the obstacles in adult life that potentially
hinder learning.

The popularity of third force psychological views in adult and
continuing education is credited as being at least partially responsible
for two programmatic components: human development or human
potential seminars as offered by a variety of business and industrial
training programs, and encounter-type groups and group therapy
sessions in such diverse settings as libraries, hospitals, factories, and
schools.

Some suggest that theories of individual value that focus sharply
upon the development of the whole person are in close harmony with

historical social and cultural values. The development of the individual is the objective of adult and continuing education programs that reflect the human values of Rogers, Maslow, Jung, and Allport.

ADULT LIFE STAGES

Research concerning adult life-stage development has opened the door to an array of programming opportunities in adult and continuing education. It promises to soon equal the attention given to human potential programs. Since Sheehy (1976) popularized the concept and Levinson et al. (1978) added scholarly respectability, adult and continuing educators have been creatively exploiting the area.

While all the educational implications of our improved understanding of adult development remain to be fully explicated, one important result is obvious. For years laymen and many scholars approached adulthood as 40 to 50 years of static and predetermined life. The recent research serves notice to educators and social scientists that adulthood is an exciting area of life to study. The increasing availability and enriched interpretation of data have confirmed the dynamic aspect of adulthood. A more enlightened view of adulthood is now possible: Adults do not have to be satisfied with the way things are because they now have reason to believe that they can change their lives.

Robert Havighurst (1964) provides the adult educator with a useful concept of human development in the Kansas City studies that led to his theory of developmental tasks. Havighurst suggests that adult and continuing educators can think about development during adulthood in two promising ways. One way is to think of the developmental tasks of the adult phase of life. Havighurst defines a *developmental task* as a task that must be achieved at an approximate phase of life if persons are to be judged and to judge themselves as competent individuals. According to the theory, failure in a developmental task is likely to be followed by failure with other tasks. Conversely, success prepares a person for successful performance of later tasks.

Three forces contribute to the emergence of a developmental task: (a) biological development, (b) social demands and expectations, and (c) ambition and aspiration. In adulthood social demands and personal aspirations dominate the setting and definitions of developmental tasks. The biological changes of middle life and later maturing probably assert a strong force after about age 50 (Havighurst, 1964).

A second way of conceptualizing development during adulthood is to think of adult life as consisting of a set of changing social roles. A *social role* is defined as a complex of behavior appropriate to a given position in social life, defined by the expectations of society and of the individual. For example, a parent is expected to behave in certain socially approved ways, and parents expect this behavior of themselves.

Havighurst's theory is sufficiently flexible to provide for variation according to one's social group. He says the above paradigm applies to North American middle-class people. It appears logical to suggest that the timing of the tasks may vary according to the demographic structure in a given period. For example, there is evidence that American middle-class young adults are now delaying marriage until later in life than did their parents and grandparents.

Recently, social scientists and educators of adults have discovered a number of other paradigms concerning development during adulthood. Popular contemporary writers on this topic include Erikson (1963), Gould (1978), Levinson et al. (1978), and Sheehy (1976). These authors have opened the door for program planners in adult and continuing education.

The ideas of life-stage development suggest program possibilities for religious organizations, business and industry, and volunteer and educational agencies. Havighurst went so far as to suggest some of the tasks that seem to be especially suitable for partial resolution through an educational activity, and Erikson's conceptualization of the interplay of successive life stages is particularly interesting. A few implications of Erikson's multidimensional theory of maturation are suggested.

1. Every educational activity provides an opportunity for growth by each individual in several dimensions. For example, although focusing on stimulating growth toward increased enlightenment, a course on world affairs can be planned so as to stimulate growth toward greater independence of thought, broader interests, and greater objectivity and tolerance for ambiguity.

2. The dimensions of maturation are interdependent so that changes in one direction affect other dimensions. For example, considerable growth toward enlightenment might be produced by methods (such as those used in the traditional lecture course) that cause the student to become increasingly dependent on the teacher. Although a choice may sometimes have to be made between such values, a truly artistic teacher will try to induce positive growth in all dimensions.

3. Every person moves on a scale from zero to infinity in each dimension throughout life and incorporates learnings from a given experience in proportion to their relevance to his or her stage of development at that moment. For example, in a group of 15 adult students, the individuals would be ready to take 15 different degrees of responsibility for their own learning. If the learning experience is to be maximally useful, provision must be made for this range of differences.

No doubt other ultimate needs could be identified, but these illustrate that the adult teacher's mission in helping individuals is far more complex and significant than it might appear on the surface.

Vivian McCoy (1977) has provided leadership in developing applied concepts and strategies for educators seeking to relate programming to life-stage development. McCoy has interpreted the work of previously mentioned scholars as addressing six specific age periods in adulthood. As conceptualized by McCoy (see table 3.1), it is evident that the idea of developmental tasks can be productively applied in programming for adult learners. Merriam and Mullins (1980), however, report some research indicating that the application of the concept to program strategies is more complex than it first appears. Merriam and Mullins found differences among the three age groups studied. They also discovered that many of the developmental tasks were not simple unitary ones but could be described as complex and correlated.

The potential programming opportunities presented by new insights concerning transitions in adulthood have not escaped the attention of educators. The work of McCoy and Merriam and Mullins barely scratches the surface of this fertile area. A number of different types of adult and continuing education programs are reported in *New Directions for Continuing Education: Programming for Adults*

TABLE 3.1: Educational Possibilities Based on the Developmental Task Concept

Developmental Stage	Tasks	Program Response	Outcomes Sought
Midlife Reexamination 35–43	1. Search for meaning 2. Reassess marriage 3. Reexamine work 4. Relate to teenage children 5. Relate to aging parents 6. Reassess personal priorities 7. Adjust to single life 8. Problem solve	1. Search for meaning workshops 2. Marriage workshops 3. Mid-career workshops 4. Parenting: focus on raising teenage children 5. Relating to aging parents workshops 6. Value clarification; goal-setting workshops 7. Living alone and divorce workshops 8. Creative problem-solving workshops	1. Coping with existential anxiety 2. Satisfying marriages 3. Appropriate career decisions 4. Improved parent-child relations 5. Improved child-parent relations 6. Autonomous behavior 7. Fulfilled single state 8. Successful problem solving
Restabilization 44–45	1. Adjust to realities of work 2. Adjust to empty nest 3. Become more deeply involved in social life 4. Participate actively in community concerns 5. Handle increased demands of older parents 6. Manage leisure time 7. Manage budget to support college-age children and ailing parents 8. Adjust to single state	1. Personal, vocational counseling, and career workshops 2. Marriage and personal counseling workshops 3. Human relations groups 4. Civic and social issues education 5. Gerontology workshops 6. Leisure use workshops 7. Financial management workshops 8. Workshops on loneliness and aloneness	1. Job adjustment 2. Exploring new sources of satisfaction 3. Effective social relations 4. Effective citizenship 5. Better personal and social adjustment of elderly 6. Creative use of leisure 7. Sound consumer behavior 8. Fulfilled single state

Note: From V. R. McCoy, Adult life cycle change, Lifelong Learning: The Adult Years, 1977, 1, 16–17. Reprinted with permission.

Facing Mid-Life Change (Knox, 1979b). Note that the examples cited in Knox's book focus on mid-life. Programs based on other life stages also present a productive area of educational activity. Furthermore, it is possible that stages and transitions currently identified as culturally inspired changes associated with social developments and technological advances will be modified in the future.

LIFELONG LEARNING

Parallel with new insights concerning adult development, a deeper and broader interest in lifelong learning is emerging. If one accepts the concept of adult development theories, it is easy to understand how some adults respond positively to suggestions concerning the importance of learning throughout life. Indeed, American history provides an ample list of individuals who have demonstrated commitment to lifelong learning. The list includes Benjamin Franklin, Cotton Mather, Catherine Schuyler, and Mercy Warren (Long, 1975). Even prior to 1900, psychologists had already turned their attention to the study of adult learning ability (Bryan & Harter, 1897, 1899), but the idea has gained increasing currency with the passage of each decade in the twentieth century.

Three areas of research in adult and continuing education provide a solid foundation for the popular acceptance of lifelong learning. The first is research concerning the adult's ability to learn. This research has progressively enhanced the perception of the adult's learning ability over the past 50 years. The second area includes the numerous participation studies that clearly reveal substantial rates of adult participation in educational activity, credit and noncredit. The third area addresses and legitimizes the self-directed learning activity of adults. The following pages discuss research in each of these areas.

LEARNING ABILITY

E. L. Thorndike's (1928) work is too well known among scholars to require extensive reporting here. Basically, he concludes that the learning ability of human beings extends beyond late adolescence. He suggests that the adult's ability to learn persists across the life-span but at a slowly declining rate of about 1 percent a year from ages 45 to 70 years. The work of Thorndike was significant for several reasons. First, he raised the age of accepted learning ability of adults and second, and perhaps of equal importance, his status as a psychologist provided a scientific basis for a movement that was already gaining momentum in American society.

Thorndike's benchmark research concerning the *rate* of adult learning was quickly followed by Irving Lorge's investigations into the *power* of adult learning ability. Lorge (Brunner et al., 1959) defines intelligence as the power to learn. Consequently, a test with time limits confuses the power to learn with the efficiency of performance. Lorge thus concluded that Thorndike's work contains some flaws that reduce the estimate of adult learning ability. Furthermore, he insisted that the quality of performance often increases with age.

The concept of lifelong learning gradually gained momentum over the four decades following the work of Thorndike and Lorge. During these years the popularity of adult and continuing education in the United States continued to increase. It was accompanied by a constantly growing body of research and foundation encouragement and governmental support. To select from a corpus of research generated over a period of 40 years is likely to be misleading. Therefore, the reader is explicitly cautioned to consider the following examples as illustrative.

Owens's (1953, 1966) studies are frequently cited as evidence of adult mental abilities. Houle (1961), who worked at about the same time as Owens, provided the field with a useful descriptive account of adult learning orientations. More recently, Baltes and Schaie (1974) have produced interesting new data based on a research design that differs from the traditional cross-sectional and longitudinal designs frequently used in studies of adult learning ability. They prefer to use the cross-sequential design, which employs elements of both the cross-sectional and longitudinal designs. They contend that through this technique, both internal and external validity are strengthened. Data generated in their cross-sequential study stimulated Baltes and Schaie to observe that adult learning ability persists at a higher level for longer than previously believed.

On another front, Horn and Cattell (1967) have been working with the concept of fluid intelligence and crystallized intelligence. They believe that fluid intelligence is biologically based whereas crystallized intelligence is socially or culturally based. Consequently, even though there is an interaction between the two kinds of intelligence, they do not necessarily show the same curve of development across the life-span. This concept is useful in relating learning ability to biological and cultural changes. For example, the literature demonstrates that certain senses lose their acuity with advancing age. Conversely, the research also documents improvement in some areas such as verbal skills. Hence, fluid intelligence is associated with the former, and crystallized intelligence is associated with the latter.

A third development concerns the work of my students in the area of adult cognition based on the theoretical positions of Jean Piaget (1971). Basically, Piaget and many of his disciples posited four levels of cognitive development, the highest of which is the formal operations stage. It was accepted that the formal operations stage is universally achieved by adolescents and that the stage persists throughout adulthood. The work of Ackerman (1978), Kuhn (1978), McCrary (1977), Mirza (1975), and others suggests that the theory needs additional testing as a number of adults do not demonstrate formal operations in selected problem-solving activities.

PARTICIPATION

For at least 200 years, American and British educators, ministers, political activists, and philanthropists have been interested in determining why adults do or do not participate in learning activities. Even though there is wide agreement that explanations for enrollment in educational activities have both psychological and social dimensions, the topic is included under psychological developments for convenience.

Despite the failure of scholars to provide a general theoretical explanation for participation of adults in learning activities, program planners have been able to observe certain demographic, psychological, and sociological variables related to enrollment. The most generally recognized variable that has some predictive value is educational achievement level; we have already noted that the higher the level of education, the greater the participation. Other variables that have been investigated with varying degrees of success include age, economic status, race, and sex. As a consequence of the research, helpful concepts concerning participation continue to emerge. Some of these concepts and research procedures are briefly discussed in the following paragraphs.

In an effort to improve the usefulness of participation studies, a number of investigators turn to factor-analytic procedures to identify what they call motivational factors in participation. From 6 to 14 factors believed to be associated with participation in adult and continuing education have been identified. These factor-analytic studies are a direct result of early work by Houle (1961), who identified three orientations toward learning: (a) "activity orientation," (b) "goal orientation," and (c) "learning orientation."

At the risk of doing violence to Houle's definition, I will briefly define each of these three orientations. First, the activity-oriented individual engages in adult and continuing education for entertainment, relief from boredom or other home or work situations, or to meet other people. Second, the individual who participates from a goal orientation does so because he or she perceives the learning activity to contribute to the achievement of a specific goal; in the language of some, the educational activity is thus instrumental. Third, the person who participates from a learning orientation is involved for the purpose of learning itself. In one sense the learner participates because he or she values knowledge for its own sake.

Six popular models for explaining and predicting participation have been developed over the past generation. Program planners should be familiar with these different theoretical explanations for participation. Long (1983) has identified these six models: (a) Aslanian and Brickell's life crisis model, (b) Bergsten's valence theory, (c) Boshier's congruence model, (d) Cross's chain-of-response (COR) model, (e) McClusky's margin theory, and (f) Miller's force field model.

Despite the range of titles attributed to these models, they contain some basic areas of agreement. For instance, they all recognize the "rational" psychological factor associated with choosing to participate or deciding against participation. Even though they do not accept the same explanation, they all acknowledge the push and pull of various factors. Ultimately, it is possible to reduce the diverse models to two related theoretical areas: Lewin's force field concept and social learning theory.

Program planners may find Aslanian and Brickell's model (1980) helpful in designing and marketing specific types of educational programs related to common areas of life change. For example, educational providers in a given geographic region experiencing significant employment shifts may find continuing education programs related to this occupationally related change attractive to large numbers of adults. At a more general social level, programming may be aimed at problems associated with single parenting, parenting in mixed families (families where children of previous marriages are involved), coping with divorce, and other family-oriented topics. There is also an obvious need for programs for individuals of both sexes who experience major shifts in careers about age 45. Here we are referring to individuals who, after 10 to 15 years of upward occupational development, discover that they are being bypassed by younger colleagues or whose occupational roles are being reduced in status as a result of other organizational changes. These employees are not interested in another job, or even in moving to another location, but they are challenged to develop a new work style and to modify their occupational expectations.

Studies of participation (Houle, 1961; Johnstone & Rivera, 1965) revealed the existence of a sizable group of learners who engaged in learning more or less independent of educational institutions. Self-directed learners thus evolved as a focus of interest among adult educators.

SELF-DIRECTED LEARNING

As a result of extensive study of self-directed learning in a number of different cultural and economic settings, planners of educational activities have become aware of this form of learning. Tough (1978) is credited with the initial study of the phenomenon of self-initiated and planned learning. According to Tough's research, individuals engage in a variety of self-directed learning formats. Consequently, it is difficult to ascertain the "typical" approach to, and design of, self-directed learning. It is clear that different individuals depend upon diverse resources. Some use printed materials; others prefer electronic materials. The amount of *planning* by the individual learner also varies. Some will use prepared learning programs while others independently identify the questions they seek to solve as well as select the resources that will help them to obtain the answers.

Future developments in self-directed learning are assured by the recognition of the fact that more adults engage in this kind of learning than in sponsored group instruction. Theoreticians and practitioners are expected to be more attentive to self-directed learning issues in the future. Theoreticians are interested in identifying and explaining the processes of self-directed learning. They are stimulated to increase knowledge of similarities and differences between independently pursued learning and the more conventionally recognized group learning. New knowledge of the topic is needed by practitioners who plan, develop, and market a range of educational formats.

HOW HUMANS THINK

The program specialist in adult and continuing education should also be acquainted with the different schools of psychology and with other psychological developments. Therefore, the second part of this chapter contains a brief overview of the three main schools of psychological thought and a discussion of emerging conceptualizations of cognitive style and brain morphology.

MAJOR PSYCHOLOGICAL CONCEPTS

The philosophical orientations of most planners of adult and continuing education programs fall into the behavioral, cognitive, or humanistic schools of psychology. Scholars who base their work in each of these schools can argue rather convincingly that great progress has been made in the research and application of their respective areas. We can find evidence of the application of theory from each school in the planning and management of adult and continuing education programs. From about 1920 to 1960, behaviorism was not seriously challenged in educational circles. Some of the outstanding personalities in the field included Watson, Guthrie, Thorndike, and, more recently, Skinner. The gestalt school, a cognitively oriented group of psychologists that emphasized the "whole" rather than the parts of a situation, slowly obtained prominence between the late 1930s and the present. After World War II, the so-called third force composed of humanistically oriented psychologists grew in public acceptance. The third force is believed to remain the smallest of the three schools in terms of adherents. However, it is probably the most visible in adult education literature.

Skinner's provocative work *Beyond Freedom and Dignity* (1971) possibly did more than any other book to popularize the behavioristic orientation. It also seems to have been the one popular work that solidified a sizable minority against the more radical principles and philosophies of behaviorism. While Skinner emerged as the spokesman for behaviorism, Rogers became known as the high priest for humanism. Ausubel, Bruner, Piaget, and others shared the limelight as representatives for the cognitive position while Gagne has kept one foot in the camps of behaviorism and cognitivism.

It is not our purpose here to discuss the merits of one of these schools over the others. Dissertations have been written on the topic, and it is unlikely that we will resolve the issue here; furthermore, it is not necessary that we do so. Each of the three schools has prospered in the last decade, and each has made important contributions to our understanding of human learning. For example, behavior modification practices have come directly from the laboratory of the behaviorist. These practices have frequently proved to be very useful for specific discrete learning tasks. Behaviorism has greatly contributed to recognition and acceptance of task analysis in many settings including continuing education programs. In turn, task analysis has improved the educator's ability to identify specific learning objectives. This then enables us to design learning activities for the achievement of selected goals.

Behaviorism has been our best source of information about learning in individualized situations where "programmed" instructional formats have proven especially useful. Because of the potential of wider and more sophisticated applications of the electronic media to adult and continuing education, it is unlikely that we shall see a complete rejection of behaviorism.

There are those, however, who feel that the school's emphasis on the external measurable aspects of behavior and rigidly set learning objectives is too restrictive. The behaviorist's refusal to examine the "black box" of the mind is perceived by some psychologists and educators as a refusal to come to grips with the most important issues in learning. The cognitive psychologists and educators believe that humans are more than a complex set of responses waiting for stimuli. They believe that the organism is an initiating entity that has the power to reason, to think, to remember, to consider, to feel, to believe, to hope, to delay gratification, to have flashes of inspiration that are difficult to explain, and to see something in the whole of a situation that makes it greater than the sum of its parts. Most of these ideas are unacceptable to the radical behaviorists. Cognitively oriented scholars and practitioners believe in concepts such as creativity and problem solving. They believe that the human is sometimes able to go beyond the information given to solve problems or to generate a new concept. These people also maintain that the cognitive ability of the human is developmental; infants, children, and young adults (possibly older ones, too) go through regular and consistent stages of mental development that help explain how we progress from handling concrete items to abstract concepts.

One of the most significant developments in the psychology of learning has been the restoration of the *mind* in learning theory. Jerome Bruner and others have conceptualized the human learning process as an active one whereby the mind provides internal structures and models of the world. This position is quite different from the traditional stimulus-response perspective that conceptualized the human organism as passive.

The action-oriented concept of the human mind yields a model of learning that significantly contrasts with the older passive model. Adult learners, according to this model, should become adept at deriving rules of behavior and applying principles. Transfer of learning and inductive processes are worthy concepts in the action-oriented model.

For a number of years, Piaget's theory (1971) that the highest level of cognitive ability was achieved by mid-adolescence was generally accepted. In the 1970s, as we noted earlier, a number of studies produced data leading to a different opinion. Long, McCrary, and Ackerman (1979) published a solid review of the literature on this topic. Based on their review, there is good reason to believe that many adults have not achieved the formal level of operations (the highest abstract level according to Piaget) and that many older adults do not necessarily routinely demonstrate formal operational behaviors based on Piaget's method of assessment. These findings have important implications for the planners of adult and continuing education activities. Many educational programs for adults are based on the manipulation of abstract symbols and the development of concepts that are abstracted from larger data bases. Failure to recognize that a sizable minority of the participants in continuing education programs lack the capability to address such abstractions will contribute to incongruence between those individuals and the content of the learning experience.

COGNITIVE STYLE AND BRAIN MORPHOLOGY

Developments in psychology with significance for the planning and operation of adult and continuing education programs are not limited to the work of the third force psychologist. Two other important areas of research and study have important implications for practitioners of the field. The two areas are concerned with the conceptualization and study of a psychological construct known as cognitive structure and a physiological or morphological construct referred to as brain lateralization.

The work in the area of cognitive style is basically concerned with the proposition that different individuals have distinctive manners, approaches, or styles of perceiving and processing information. At least nine different cognitive styles have been identified in the literature.

1. Field independence versus field dependence is described as an analytical versus a global way of perceiving.
2. Scanning is described as a way of attending to phenomena.
3. Breadth of categorizing refers to a preference for establishing categories (broad or narrow).
4. Conceptualizing styles refer to ways of selecting information for concept differentiation or formation of concepts.
5. Cognitive complexity versus simplicity refers to individual differences in ways of construing the world, particularly the world of social behavior.
6. Reflectiveness versus impulsivity refers to the speed with which individuals tend to act on problems, hypotheses, and information.

7. Leveling versus sharpening refers to consistent tendencies in assimilation in memory.
8. Constricted versus flexible control refers to susceptibility to distraction and cognitive interference.
9. Tolerance for incongruous or unrealistic experiences refers to the ability to accept perceptions that vary from conventional experience (Cross, 1976, pp. 114–15).

The bulk of the research concerning cognitive styles remains in the theoretical area although a number of studies relate cognitive styles as measured on appropriate instruments to occupational activities and problem-solving approaches. The theoretical area has important implications for the planning and practice of adult and continuing education. For example, for years educators have been studying the relative efficacy of different techniques. There is increasing recognition that such comparative studies will produce little information that can be used in planning instructional strategies. The theoretical trend favors the proposition that individuals have distinctive cognitive styles and that they accordingly will interact with different educational techniques in a manner consistent with the dominant cognitive style they possess. If this proposition holds true, then educators who have for years attempted to individualize instructional and learning activities will find themselves challenged to do more prescriptive planning.

As of this date, there is little in the literature to inform the practitioner of the relative usefulness of a given educational technique for individuals who are identified as preferring a field-independent cognitive style as opposed to a field-dependent style. Similarly, there is little assistance available in the literature for those individuals who have been identified as preferring cognitive processes that result in "leveling versus sharpening." The absence of useful research in this area does not reduce the significance of the implications for the practice of adult and continuing education.

Research in the area of brain lateralization is also of potential significance for practitioners in adult and continuing education. Brain lateralization research is concerned with the concept of right and left hemispheres of the brain. Proponents of brain lateralization believe that the right and left hemispheres have highly specialized functions. For example, most right-handed individuals are considered to be dominated by the left side of the brain as opposed to the right side. The left hemisphere is identified with the development of language, logic, and rationality in contrast to the right hemisphere, which is identified with melody, intuition, and spatial concepts. The literature on this topic generally cites the need for educators to become aware of the different functions of the two hemispheres and to provide learning experiences that involve functions of each. Western education is criticized as favoring the left side of the brain to the exclusion of the right side.

This topic is replete with speculations, propositions, and conjectures that require additional testing. It is also in danger of becoming one of the fads for which education is famous.

Other developments related to the morphology and physiology of the brain include research with various chemicals. Such research is based upon the premise that the brain is an electrochemical organ that interacts with other electrochemical organs of the body. For example, there is evidence that certain proteins or carbohydrates help raise or decrease levels of chemicals in the bloodstream. These chemicals in turn interact with structural components of the brain and nervous system to either stimulate or repress other electrochemical processes. In some studies the selected chemical agent may be directly injected in the bloodstream to measure its impact on behavior. Consequently, certain kinds of cognitive activity, such as memory, have been associated with electrochemical processes. Based on the research that has tied certain kinds of memory behavior to particular chemical elements, futurists have suggested the possibility of development of a memory pill or some other kind of treatment to improve mental functioning.

While much of the work in this area also remains at the theoretical level, it is possible to see how learners and administrators of adult and continuing education programs might be influenced by future developments. For example, we may discover that meals provided at conferences contain the wrong kinds of food to stimulate or enhance learning activities. We may also discover that learners who are having difficulty with certain behaviors may be in some way helped by a correct diet. We may even find ways to offset the fatigue that often hinders adult learners in late-hour educational activities.

Some practitioners today may believe these developments have limited implications for the practice of adult and continuing education, but we should remember that space travel, intercontinental warfare, and satellite telecommunication circuitry were equally far-fetched ideas less than 50 years ago.

SUMMARY AND CONCLUSIONS

At least three different kinds of psychological developments important to planners of adult education programs have occurred in recent years. Each has potential significance for the development and management of adult and continuing education activities. The first concerns what I have called a *mind-set*. The second development is related to our increasing knowledge of adult participation in learning. And the third psychological development concerns the evolvement of psychological theories and their application to learning, thinking, and behaving.

Based on the content of this chapter, it is apparent that frames of reference or mind-set varies among generations. Twentieth-century children and their parents have reached maturity in different cultures even though they live their lives in the same geographical region. Changes in culture and views of self-in-the-world are associated with educational attitudes, beliefs, and values. Educators of adults must be sensitive to such psychological developments.

Research in adult life-stage development also should encourage us concerning the possibility of modifications of the me generation's self-centered concerns. We are informed that mind transformation is a critical element in some humanistically oriented learning today. Therefore, mind transformation may also be successfully applied in the adult learning environment. Stage development–related crises will, of course, be faced and addressed in different ways. There is reason to believe that some of the baby boom generation will turn to adult and continuing education as a means for addressing and resolving such crises.

Study of cognitive styles and brain morphology provides incomplete but stimulating results. If we can discover ways to apply the emerging knowledge about cognitive styles and brain morphology for educational purposes, we may be able to meet the adult and continuing education needs of the younger adult population despite negativism that might counter improved attitudes toward lifelong learning.

IMPLICATIONS

Developments of a psychological nature as identified in this chapter pose interesting implications for program activity in adult and continuing education. For example, a prevailing social attitude favorable to lifelong learning improves the general potential for adult and continuing education program success: a marketing concern. A second implication is in the "delivery" and structure of the programs as well as content and audience elements: use of new technology in self-directed as well as in sponsored group learning activities, for example.

Since the late sixties, personal self-improvement activities have been popular with adults. These programs have taken literally hundreds of different formats from group therapy sessions, limited to a small number of participants, to gigantic conferences held in large municipal convention centers. The content ranges over an equally diverse spectrum from the human potential movement to secular and religious emphases on family and marriage enrichment. The design and instructional resources employed in the educational activities mentioned here fall along a continuum that reflects extreme degrees of sophistication. Some reflect an eclectic approach to learning theory. Others tend toward humanistic or behavioristic philosophies.

Recognition of self-directed learning as a popular and legitimate way for adults to continue their education also will likely affect adult education in a number of ways. There are implications for philosophy as well as practice. Educators will continue to seek to integrate concepts of various formats of learning into their philosophy. In addition, practical implications must be considered as the practice of self-directed learning is integrated with, or stands in opposition to, the conventional sponsored group formats. The media technology and administrative and educational technology discussed elsewhere in this book must be matched with developments in self-directed learning.

4 Developments in Electronic Media Technology

We have seen that administrators and planners of educational programs for adults are constrained by various social and psychological developments. These phenomena impinge upon the processes and consequences of program-planning procedures in diverse and unpredictable ways. Simultaneously, they constitute a source that will reward creativity, imagination, and originality in the program-planning process. Advances in electronic media technology and the general distribution of sophisticated electronic devices among Americans also present new and challenging opportunities for planners of adult education programs.

Because of the speed at which innovations are taking place, any listing of media is likely to be incomplete by publication date. Thus, the following list is only illustrative. Some of the developments include:

- Electronic blackboards
- Electronic mail
- Fiber optics
- Satellite circuitry
- Slow-scan television
- Television disc players
- Interactive television

- Micro audio cassette recorder players
- Micro data processors
- Miniaturization
- Television recorder players
- Word processors

Technological developments represent one of the most challenging areas in programming in adult and continuing education. Advances that may have educational applications occur with such speed that it is difficult for the adult and continuing educator to keep abreast of them. At this writing one of the newest devices touted for educational use is the "electronic blackboard." It is one of the most recent additions to the rapidly developing inventory of devices available for use in teleconferencing. Yet, by the time this book is published, it is likely that newer and improved versions of this remarkable instrument will be available for educators to consider.

Educators of adults, regardless of their institutional role and mission, find the processes and promises of technology particularly confounding. Most educators of adults seem fairly well prepared to contend with the issues and questions represented by social and psychological developments. This does not seem to be the case where technology is concerned. For example, we have not mastered the use of some of the less sophisticated media such as films, filmstrips, audiotapes, and radio. Uncertainty about these media interferes with acceptance of the more sophisticated ones. Second, educational budgets are so low that preparatory programs for adult education professionals usually cannot employ the best and most modern devices. Similarly, operating budgets are usually too low to provide adequate equipment for delivering educational service through advanced media such as television and computer hookups.

The potential scope of adult and continuing education through the application of the electronic media is revealed by a recent report on its use in California (California Postsecondary Education Commission, 1979). The commission reports that over 50,000 Californians enroll each year in broadcast telecourses for academic credit, and well over 60,000 utilize video and audio cassettes for continuing professional education beyond the classroom. Included are attorneys, registered nurses, and physicians. Increasingly, other linkages are providing formal learning opportunities in other than classroom modes. Such services are as follows: instructional television fixed systems (ITFS) linking campuses with offices, learning centers, hospitals and homes; newspaper lecture series; and radio broadcasts. While other media are also being explored, professionals have used these for several years to remain competent and competitive. According to the California Postsecondary Education Commission, these newer modes of learning have successfully enrolled additional thousands who would not have taken regular campus classroom courses.

Despite the appearance of success with electronic media in California, the commission reports a number of challenges that must be resolved. Such challenges concern issues of fees, state support, interinstitutional cooperation, and geographic equity in the availability of learning opportunities. An illustration is found in the commission's observation that colleges have selected courses for broadcast according to a "marketing" model rather than a "curriculum" model. Hence, it describes the broadcast offerings as having an "ad hoc" character (p. iii).

Technology has affected programming in adult and continuing education in at least three different ways.

1. Technological change has pervaded society. Its consequences have become associated with some of the social changes discussed in chapter 2. Workplaces have been changed and employment skills modified, new knowledge has been required, and people have learned new ways to relate to each other and to different information sources. The cumulative effects of these technologically stimulated and based changes have placed additional learning requirements on adults. The additional learning requirements in turn have contributed to innovative programming in adult and continuing education.

2. Technological change has resulted in new administrative processes and procedures in the field of adult and continuing education, or it has caused changes in other spheres of life that affect the management of the field. This kind of technological impact is discussed in chapter 5.

3. The third kind of technological change, and the one with which we are concerned in this chapter, is related to equipment, devices, structures, and social relationships flowing out of the new devices that have direct application in the processes of planning and implementing adult and continuing education. For example, interactive television and computers provide an opportunity for different kinds of relationships *between* instructors and learners as well as interaction *among* learners. These devices also have implications for "institutional" relationships.

Previously we examined social and psychological developments that are likely to affect the creation and management of continuing education programs. While occurrences specific to both of these areas of change contribute to some uncertainties and the possibility of writing alternative scenarios, the range of unknowns is equally great in the area of technological developments. The literature available on the "new" media and education contains a number of questions, countless propositions, and untold promises. Prophets in the area are as numerous as ants at a picnic, and it appears that they have all taken an oath of disagreement. The failure of specialists in the media and technology to agree on specific future applications of telecommunications devices and computers, however, does not reduce the significance of their potential impact on continuing education in the years ahead.

Recent advancements—computer graphics, interactive systems, microcomputers, satellite and telephone line transmission, videodiscs, and videotapes—boggle the mind with the potential of previously unthinkable applications to adult and continuing education. Unfortunately, many of us do not even know the right questions to ask, and we are even less likely to know how to apply the electronic media.

Even though there are questions about how and under what kinds of circumstances to use the new media, there is recognition that they can provide many benefits, including the following:

- Better access to instruction for the less mobile—from the handicapped to the full-time worker with family responsibilities
- Energy savings from less dependence on the automobile and the classroom
- Alternative, less costly methods for continuing professional education
- Encounters with leading scholars and practitioners in various fields
- More opportunity for individual attention from the on-campus instructor
- Opportunity for repetition of instruction, with less reliance on note taking and more chance of mastery learning
- The possibility of individualizing programs, thereby increasing learner persistence
- A wider audience of "adjunct learners"—those who do not enroll but follow the course and perhaps become interested in later activities
- Lower public cost per enrolled student (California Postsecondary Education Commission, 1979)

This chapter addresses four topics of interest to the continuing educator: (a) a clarification of terms, (b) a brief historical overview, (c) a discussion of selected technology, and (d) some questions that remain to be answered.

TERMINOLOGY

A medium may be defined as any kind of device that is normally used to transmit information between two or more people. An educational medium is such a device used for educational purposes. Printed materials such as books, pamphlets, diagrams, and maps are all educational media, as are globes, artifacts, language laboratories, radio, and television. When telecommunications devices are used for educational purposes, they also become educational media. At other times they may serve as business or entertainment media.

Biddle and Rossi (1967) note that media are devices and the appearance of a new medium always constitutes a technological innovation. In this sense then, new telecommunications advances constitute innovations that ultimately affect the social order and community life and behavior. The effects of educational media are not always easy to predict, but is generally agreed that in the form of telecommunications devices, they tend to enlarge individual and social horizons.

Technology is not an educational medium. It is the science of the application of knowledge to practical purposes. Thus, theoretically, technology contributes to the invention and creation of devices and procedures. Educational technology is the science of the application of knowledge for the purpose of improving the educational process. Knowledge of the telecommunications and computer devices and processes discussed in the following pages can be employed to fashion them into educational media.

HISTORICAL OVERVIEW

The history of educational applications of technology is rather dismal. The first teaching machines as contemporarily conceptualized were manufactured commercially as early as 1928 (Balanoff, 1967). The roots of programmed instruction lie mainly in psychology and educational psychology and date from the early work of Pressey in the 1920s. The teaching machine was perceived as a way to either test students' knowledge or provide them with immediate knowledge of results when used in instruction (Strolurow, 1967).

Military applications provided an impetus for broader applications of different media for educational purposes. The applications included simulated motors and other equipment on which inexperienced mechanics worked to diagnose and correct malfunctions (Hechinger, 1980). The idea of the link trainer, developed during World War II to teach certain skills to air force pilots, later found substance in similar machines for the training of helicopter pilots and astronauts.

Under the pressure of the postwar baby boom upon schools, educators turned to technology for help. The Foundation for the Advancement of Education, a subsidiary of the Ford Foundation, focused on television as a potential adjunct to classroom education. Instructional television, however, was sometimes cast in a role that threatened educators. For example, the entire school district of Hagerstown, Maryland, was wired for closed-circuit instructional television. The plan was for the teachers to produce their lessons in special studios for broadcasting into classrooms for repeated use over several years or with several groups of children.

Other innovations that gained some attention during the period included language laboratories with individual listening and talking booths. These advances were commonly perceived as general cures for many educational ills. Unfortunately, the early experience with educational technology proved to be disappointing for a number of reasons. Hechinger identifies five reasons for the lack of success of educational technology:

1. The manufacturers of the hardware proved more sophisticated than the producers of software, the actual teaching materials to be fed into machines.
2. Producing effective software to answer the varied needs of the classroom called for writing and editing skills which were in short supply.
3. Competing producers of hardware made their products incompatible with software production of competitors, thus raising the cost to the consumer.
4. Educators often approached the technology with doubts or even open hostility, fearing that the machine might be used

to replace the teacher, even though the intention of the inno-
vators was primarily to make teachers more effective.

5. The machinery often required too much technological sophistication (which school people lacked) and costly maintenance.
(1980, p. 6)

Despite problems associated with faculty suspicion, institutional
rigidity, and other factors, the new media continued to be advocated
as significant additions to the classroom. Encyclopaedia Britannica
Films, for example, is cited for outstanding cinematic productions
with scholarly commentary (Hechinger, 1980). Public television is
credited with "Sesame Street" and "The Electric Company" while
commercial television provided "Sunrise Semester" and "Summer
Semester."

Other successful applications of technology include the audiotape cassette program at UCLA for subscribing physicians. The State
University of New York at Buffalo is recognized for special radio
programs for physicians broadcast on assigned wavelengths. And in
the 1970s, Britain's Open University, which combines television,
radio, and print in its highly visible program, had its impact on
American educators.

Thus, even though the period from World War II until the early
1980s is often perceived negatively when technology and the new
educational media are discussed, some see the future in brighter tones.
Hechinger (1980) believes that the use of technology is in its in-
fancy. Furthermore, he is convinced that the 1980s will be able to
build upon the experiences just noted. With such a foundation,
greater and faster progress is likely in the immediate future. Hechinger cites four reasons for such optimism:

1. The production of the necessary hardware at an affordable
price is now technically possible.
2. The need for continued education, particularly in fast moving
vocations and professions, is greater than ever, and increasing
numbers of people will want to update their skills but do so
on their own time outside formal institutions.
3. Young teachers who are entering the schools are themselves
a part of the television generation and computers and, in contrast to their predecessors, neither hostile to, nor afraid of, television, computers, and technology in general. Many schools
and colleges are now teaching computer science. . . .
4. Entirely new fields, moreover, are beginning to open up. For
example, the video disk, which is already being test-marketed,

can be expected soon to offer to education in and out of school and campus, a previously unheard of variety of video-recorded materials available for instant and repeated viewing. Information banks are already in an advanced stage of commercial availability to provide background and reference materials on virtually every subject in a matter of minutes. The home terminal which will provide printouts of research papers is believed by many experts to be just around the corner.

(Hechinger, 1980, pp. 9–10)

SELECTED MEDIA IN CONTINUING EDUCATION

The electronic media available for application in continuing education include six major telecommunications delivery technologies: (a) public broadcasting (radio and TV), (b) instructional television fixed services (ITFS), (c) teleconferencing-telewriting (via standard telephone circuits), (d) FM Broadcasting station multiplexity, (e) community antenna television (CATV), and (f) satellite circuitry (Curtis, 1979). Other related devices include computers for computer-assisted learning and computer-managed instruction, videodiscs and players, videotape recorder players and tapes, audiotape recorder players, newspapers, and other print media. Because of space limitations, only selected media applications are discussed on the following pages.

All of these items are currently in use to meet educational objectives, and most of them have contemporary continuing education applications. The justifications for resorting to electronic media to supplement, enrich, or replace some elements of the traditional teaching-learning transaction are numerous and tend to reflect the values and biases of the providers. The rationales include (a) rising per-student costs, (b) increasing costs of transportation incurred directly by the student or the organization that supports the educational activity, and (c) effectiveness of the new technologies and media.

VIDEO TECHNOLOGY

Cable television and satellite circuitry are the "new kids on the block." Even though they have been around for several years, they are often mentioned when applications to continuing education are discussed. While they reflect fundamental differences in broadcast technology—land lines and circuitry employ electronic signals transmitted via an orbiting satellite to a TVRO (television receiving only) "dish"—these media are potential competitors for the same market. Today there are a variety of combinations: (a) transmission limited to land lines (cable), (b) land lines in combination with TVRO dishes, and (c) direct reception via the TVRO by the user. At first only cable companies could afford to purchase the TVRO dishes, but current technology reduced the cost from $75,000 in 1976 to $15,000 in 1979. There is the possibility of eventual conflict between the cable companies and individuals or organizations who wish to purchase TVRO service instead of cable service. The issue will likely emerge full-blown when Comsat launches its satellite-to-home pay-TV service. Such a system is already being put into place in Japan (Smith, 1981).

Advances in satellite circuitry have contributed to the emerging teleconferencing concept. Teleconferencing based on the telephone has been relatively popular for a number of years. The technology of satellite broadcasts, however, has enhanced the possibility of televised teleconferences over the land lines formerly used. The Holiday Inn Corporation has moved into the teleconferencing activity with enthusiasm. By the middle of 1983 the corporation had 320 earth stations in 42 states tied into its satellite-based structure (Hayes, 1983). One corporate executive who used the Holiday Inn network (Bean, n.d.) estimated that a 1980 conference cost $100,000 compared with $500,000 for a similar centralized conference in 1972.

Compared to the excitement generated by the promises of cable television and satellite circuitry, the telephone (audio only) teleconferencing system stimulates little passion. However, audio teleconferencing has great potential and an apparently sound track record. The steadily increasing costs of transportation have nudged organizations to look to teleconferencing as a means of staff development at decentralized locations. Because it is based on standard telephone lines, accessibility is almost universally possible in the United States. High costs such as those encountered with some TV productions are reduced, or expenses are generally limited to the fee for the telephone service, printed materials, and consultants (if used). The existence of a few learners at each of several locations reduces the problems associated with low enrollment at a central location and meets the educational needs of the isolated practitioner in less populated areas.

Timing is one of the difficulties encountered with many mass broadcast educational activities. An excellent and highly desirable educational program broadcast at 8:00 P.M. on any day of the week automatically excludes a number of potential viewers who are regularly or temporarily unavailable at the broadcast time. The videotape recorder is touted as a technological corrective. The device will permit John and Mary Smith to record a particular program at any time, even while they attend their local PTA meeting or religious service.

The videotape recorder player and the videodiscs are potential supplements to the ubiquitous audiotape. Cost differences between the tapes and discs and playback equipment will likely lead to selective use. For example, it is believed that the videodisc player will soon be available for $400 or less, and two-hour discs will be available for $15. Videotape recorder players are also projected to become available for approximately $400, with prerecorded tapes selling for about $30. The tapes and discs also have other different features such as the higher sound quality that makes the videodiscs attractive for foreign language, music, and certain science courses.

Rapid developments in the technology of video recording and playback devices change this area weekly. Most large urban centers in North America now have dealers who engage in renting or buy-back arrangements. Thus, videodiscs featuring popular current movies are available at less cost than an evening at the movies. Advances in linking the computer's rapid scan potential with videodiscs also represent significant possibilities for their use as reference material.

The relationships among the various electronic media—radio, television, and computers—have contributed to the "TV component" approach to developing home "systems." Audio on quality FM equipment greatly enhances the TV video signals. Successful integration of the various components promises to open yet another door to broadcast, storage, and playback possibilities.

COMPUTERS

The revolutionary progress in telecommunication is matched by similar progress in the computer field. Operational diversity and speed have increased at the same time that computer size and costs have decreased. Thus, the possibility of a computer in every home becomes increasingly likely. Well over a million microcomputers for home use have already been sold, and the upward sales curve and downward price trends are continuing (Smith, 1981). Home computers can now be linked to different data banks for nominal hookup and service fees. For example, one service charges $100.00 for a hookup fee, and subscribers can access information in the bank for $15.00 during the day or $2.75 per hour in the evening (Smith, 1981). The home computer has a variety of educational applications in areas as diverse as word processing, language skills, geometry, and so forth. New programs for educational application are becoming available on a regular basis.

ITFS

Instructional television fixed service (ITFS) is in effect a closed-circuit delivery system using the airwaves to connect a central transmitting point with one or more designated receiving points. It cannot reach the public outside of specified receiving points such as classrooms or learning centers. In essence, ITFS permits an institution to transmit its regular campus classroom instruction to other locations.

The California experience with remote instruction shows the potential of the electronic media for use in education. In sparsely settled northeastern California, for example, one or more persons can participate in a class at the Chico campus of the state university by going to one of six regional learning centers located in various communities in the area. Each learning center has a classroom equipped to receive the ITFS signal, and the student can respond live to the professor by telephone. Since the educational institution and faculty retain control over the entire situation, including the broadcast and who can watch it, educators feel little constraint to adapt their classroom teaching either to a new medium or to a new or different potential target audience. One Chico professor has stated that "every effort is made to encourage faculty to treat an ITFS delivered course in the same way (or nearly so) as a non-ITFS course" (California Postsecondary Education Commission, 1979, p. 6). It is believed that this approach helps to resolve two problems: faculty participate more readily, and the institution extends its outreach. It also avoids the expenditure of planning and coordinating tapes required for taped telecourses, an expense that includes a heavy drain on faculty time.

The combination of ITFS with microwave links also unites the Davis campus with the Lawrence Laboratories at Livermore, California, and several state government buildings in Sacramento. Eleven California hospitals are linked by ITFS with university campuses. The Stanford University School of Engineering uses a four-channel ITFS system with interactive capability to provide instruction to more than 30 firms located on the San Francisco Peninsula. With three other universities, the Stanford network enrolled over 3,600 students in a recent 12-month period. San Diego University is also in the process of establishing a video link between its main campus and the adjunct campus at Calexico.

A staff member of the state university TV station, KPBS, recently received a training grant for public broadcasting and will direct a new Educational and Special Services Office within KPBS. Her role is to develop new ways to serve special groups in San Diego by the transmission of educational programs from the San Diego campus to specific locations. The deaf constitute a target group appropriate for new uses of ITFS; blind people already have begun to receive educational radio programs.

COURSES BY RADIO

Even though the educational potential for radio has long been recognized by educators, its history as an educational medium is mixed. The California Postsecondary Educational Commission (1979) provides some interesting information on the use of educational radio in California.

Courses by radio in 1977–1978 took two interesting turns in California. The state university station, KPBS-FM in San Diego, broadcast two complete courses—one in political science and the other in sociology—for the severely handicapped. Each series consisted of 30 programs of 50 minutes each. Using a specially designated sub-channel, the station also airs a full weekly schedule of programming for the physically disabled that includes readings of newspapers, fiction, and nonfiction. A special receiver is required for this service, but anyone within the broadcast area may apply for the use of such a receiver.

Station KERS-FM at California State University, Sacramento, also broadcast a credit course in 1977–1978. A yet different use of radio is demonstrated by KVCR-FM at San Bernardino Valley College. This public FM radio station broadcasts 10 programs of 60 minutes each to provide high fidelity sound backup for the music course delivered by instructional TV (ITV).

The wedding of TV, radio, and print media into an instructional medium has been amply demonstrated by the Open University in Great Britain. The interested reader is referred to the numerous publications that describe the unusual success of that institution (Ferguson, 1975; Perry, 1976).

ELECTRONIC TESTING

Yet another example of new applications of electronic media to education is provided by the Educational Testing Service. ETS has recently announced its pioneering efforts with videotesting (Educational Testing Service, 1980). Much of the reported activity has been conducted in two research projects using English proficiency tests as the basis for study. The objectives of the research are to develop ways to use videotesting to simplify, speed delivery, and overcome the security problems inherent in mailing large numbers of examinations all over the world.

One of the experimental projects resulted in the creation of a test of English proficiency for computer transmission, via telephone line, undersea cable, or satellite, to appear on TV monitors before 100 volunteer test takers in the Netherlands. ETS reports that in addition to testing the feasibility of long-distance transmission, the experiment will investigate the impact of videotesting on performance. Subjects will take both the video and booklet forms of the test to determine if videotesting alters results (Educational Testing Service, 1980).

The other experimental project reported by ETS is work with an entirely new method of presenting the Test of English as a Foreign Language (TOEFL). A version of TOEFL has been created specifically for videotesting. This version is based entirely on one topic, and test takers are given information through a simulated lecture by a university professor, film clips, a simulated student seminar, and a regular test booklet. One pilot administration of the exam has been conducted, and a second one is in the planning stages (Educational Testing Service, 1980).

Telephone

Basic two-way communication by telephone also seems to have a yet undeveloped potential. Although distance teaching-learning programs often include the telephone and/or cassette recordings, the dominant use of the telephone has been for counseling rather than for instruction. Limited research on the use of the telephone for instruction is available. Robinson's (1981) review of its use in the open university describes several formats based on the telephone. The potential of the telephone for instruction is illustrated by recently organized foreign language courses based on its use. This system provides a teacher who calls a learner each day at a prearranged time for a 30-minute lesson. Neither the teacher nor the learner loses valuable time traveling from one location to another. The conventional lessons are supplemented by written assignments that the learner pursues between telephone lessons. This model should be conducive to the extension of telephone instruction to include more than one learner and a variety of dial-access possibilities using prerecorded instruction. For example, Tom Jones is called by his "teacher," a prerecorded tape, through an electronic procedure. Jones's comments are in turn recorded for electronic analysis of vocabulary, grammar, and other critical elements. The analysis is available in printout and audio form before the next lesson. Imagine this process multiplied by tens of students, and the potential of the system is evident.

UNANSWERED QUESTIONS

The topic of technology in education presents continuing educators with more questions than answers. Furthermore, the rapidly changing state of the art suggests that questions of today may be moot by tomorrow. Technical advances may obviate the need for answering some questions while others may increase in significance. We cannot, however, permit this state of affairs to freeze us into inactivity.

Some of the questions have been already alluded to, such as what kind of impact will satellite circuitry and inexpensive TVROs have on cable television? What are the basic instructional advantages and disadvantages of the two systems? How will educators fare in future allocations of TV cable channels?

The last question is also related to programming skills and other resources. Educators have not won many laurels through their current and previous use of television for instructional purposes. How can the requisite competencies for optional use of electronic media be developed and applied in contemporary education? Or, a more basic question, what fundamental competencies do educators need to exploit the electronic media?

Bonham (1981) has identified 10 basic questions that illustrate the kinds of issues that need examination. He concludes that educators who plan to use electronic and other technology in adult education should be concerned with such issues as barriers, audience size, demographic and psychosocial characteristics, interests, costs associated with production and delivery, and learning-teaching theories. The reader will be quick to observe that these questions are very similar to those generally raised by planners and administrators in adult and continuing education.

These and other questions concerning the application of developing electronic media represent a significant challenge for continuing educators. Some practitioners feel threatened by the technical aspects of electronic devices. Other educators believe the problems are best attended to by engineers, and they have therefore neglected some of the issues. Continued avoidance of the questions, however, must come to an end if continuing educators are to make effective use of the electronic media.

SUMMARY AND CONCLUSIONS

This chapter addresses several important topics concerned with developments in electronic media. In the introduction it is noted that although progress in a number of areas has expanded the possibilities of educational utilization, application has been slow to occur. Among the topics addressed are terminology, history, and selected media. Some specific applications such as video technology and computers are discussed, as are a few examples of media applications including the use of ITFS, radio, electronic testing capabilities, and the telephone. Finally, a number of important but unanswered questions concerning the application of electronic media in adult and continuing education are noted.

Six conclusions emerge from the content of this chapter:

1. The term *educational technology* is frequently used in inconsistent ways.
2. Historically, educational technology has not usually lived up to expectations, but many improvements are predicted.
3. A variety of electronic media have potential for educational applications.
4. The use of electronic media in education has proved to be successful in a few instances.
5. Telephone and radio seem to be receiving additional attention because of their great potential.
6. Adult educators are particularly challenged to strengthen (or develop) personal and institutional capabilities to improve the use of electronic media in adult and continuing education.

IMPLICATIONS

The electronic media discussed in this chapter pose some interesting implications for adult and continuing education. Video devices, for example, now make it possible for a single source of information (mentor) to be used by millions of learners at their own convenient time and place. How will this flexibility affect the traditional learner-instructional framework? How will certain educational institutions develop to certify the learning of a population of electronically tutored students? How will the assessment and certification be done? Why can't it too be accomplished by use of devices such as the computer?

The increasing availability and presence of the electronic media place a demand on each person to become better informed—"more literate"—concerning these media and their possible influences. For example, one president of a major university has decreed that all administrators must become better informed about the computer. Linkages between the computer, satellites, and television place an increased premium on additional understanding by a large number of people.

As more people become better informed about the possibilities of the electronic media, they will identify new applications to the learning needs of adults. Not only may computers become master teachers available at all hours of the day or night, but they may also diagnose educational needs that may not be revealed through contemporary methods of needs-assessment. The media are likely to continue to have an increasing impact on adult and continuing education activities. Administrative processes, marketing, instruction, and instructional management are just a few of the areas that are sensitive to influence from the media.

We have discussed how the electronic media will free the learner. The ability to receive and store information for repeated use, or for use at a more convenient time, will also free the programmer. Similar flexibility will relieve participants of pressures to "attend" a conference or meeting or educational activity at some distant location where travel often requires as much as 50 percent of the time occupied by the learning activity itself.

Computer graphics and other advances in interactive modes promise to open the way to skill-learning activities that heretofore required expensive shops and equipment. We noted earlier how mechanics in the military used simulated equipment to diagnose malfunctions. Automotive, small appliance, and electronic repairs along with other crafts and skills are possible topics for the application of the electronic media.

The new electronic media will influence program-planning and program-development strategies. Most adult and continuing education personnel seem to agree on a general program-planning format that has evolved from long practice. How will the new media alter the process? Involvement of representatives of the target audience may be affected in some way. For example, representatives of the target population may become more deeply involved in the development and presentation of content. Similarly, identification of resources and budgeting processes may also take on different dimensions as new procedures are developed to account for the large initial investment required for some program materials. Ways to spread the costs over several years may be needed.

Some of these ideas are related to the recommendations and questions identified in the preceding sections. They remain, however, to be developed through careful and intensive analysis.

5 Technological Developments in Administration and Education

Technological developments in administration of adult and continuing education processes that may influence programming include the following:

- Focus on Japanese management styles including quality circle concepts
- Greater use of computers, word processing, and the conference telephone in management
- Improved research technology in adult and continuing education
- Continuously changing technology of instruction, needs-assessment, and evaluation

The preceding chapters show that programming in adult and continuing education is influenced by a number of variables external to the administrator responsible for the program. A second and equally important dimension of the process, which should be made explicit here, is internal. Heretofore, with the exception of chapter 1, the discussion has focused on those larger events in society that in some way trigger participation in adult and continuing education. It is unlikely, however, that successful programs can be developed simply because there is a need for them. For example, we can all agree that a need exists for the prevention and cure of diseases such as cancer and heart disease. Even though millions of dollars are spent annually in an effort to meet these health needs, we have not been successful because important pieces of knowledge are missing. Current technology enables ear surgeons to replace tiny and important parts of the inner ear with ceramic substitutes, but no manufacturer of the items is presently available. Developments as discussed in chapters 2, 3, and 4 contribute to a fertile milieu in which the creative and insightful educator of adults may be successful. On the other hand, less creative and skillful individuals may not be optimally rewarded for a number of reasons. One important variable in program success is administrative skill or a technology of adult and continuing education.

In less complex times, when the clock seemed to tick a little slower, administrators of adult and continuing education had the luxury of learning their craft by trial and error and apprenticeship. Today there is an urgent demand for a technology of administration and instruction. There is some evidence in the literature that such a technology is slowly developing (Long, 1983). It appears that the graduate programs in adult and continuing education in major American and Canadian universities are moving toward an educational experience based on a technology of administration and instruction. The trend has been slow to develop and is often without apparent direction and marked with controversy. Nevertheless, it seems to be taking on form and substance.

Adult and continuing educators have had to win their positions against a number of odds. There has been a historical tendency for administrators to place adult and continuing education units under the supervision of individuals whose education did not reflect an understanding of the nature of adult learning activities. However, the constantly expanding group of professionally prepared educators of adults suggests that some employers prefer to employ people with graduate degrees in adult education. Many of the graduate programs, such as those at Florida State University, North Carolina State University, and the University of Wisconsin, have emphasized administrative skills development.

Obviously, concepts of graduate curricula and administration in adult and continuing education have changed in the past decade. The increasing maturity of adult and continuing education as a field of

university study has contributed to a gradual sharpening and modification of the curriculum. Simultaneously, concepts of administration,
particularly management, have benefited from research concerning
leadership styles and other important subjects. Selected topics related
to administrative and educational developments that have implications for programming in adult and continuing education are discussed in this chapter.

The administration of adult and continuing education programs
includes a variety of discrete and related activities. There is a rather
consistent dialogue in the literature of the field concerning administration. The published conversation relates to several topics: the kinds
of skills needed by adult educators; the kinds of educational programs
required to equip competent adults; and the kinds of barriers that
interfere with the optimal functioning of educators of adults in various
settings.

We have noted that the competencies of practitioners are important factors in the creation and implementation of educational
programs for adults. The attributes and abilities of administrators
and program planners are critical variables in the identification, interpretation, and translation of social, psychological, and media technology into educational program format. The sensitivities and skills
developed in graduate programs of study constitute a part of the
technology of adult and continuing education that must be brought
to bear on the complex and rapidly changing context of program
development.

The literature concerning the technology of administration
among educators of adults often includes five themes: (a) appropriate preparation, (b) the content of adult and continuing education,
(c) administrative competencies, (d) marketing, and (e) obstacles to
program development. The literature indicates that some trends may
be developing in these areas. Each of the topics is examined in the
following paragraphs.

PREPARATION OF ADULT EDUCATORS

The discussion about whom to employ as an educator of adults takes
into account several related variables. One of the first is the diversity
of the field. As noted in chapter 1, the education of adults occurs in

all kinds of agency, organizational, and institutional frameworks. In some organizations adult education is a primary task; in some it is incidental to other missions. Naturally, in agencies with a limited commitment to educational programming for adults, the need for a specialist in the field is not great. In other agencies, such as some corporations, training budgets for adults may be extremely large. Nevertheless, corporate personnel development concepts dictate that management personnel be rotated through the training division en route to other management positions. Therefore, few specialists in adult and continuing education are likely to be employed in such settings. On the other hand, governmental training programs, some health and voluntary organizations, and defense and educational organizations have identified the adult education specialist as a critical employee. The situation in postsecondary education, however, is particularly revealing on this point.

There is little doubt that continuing education units of postsecondary institutions have been regularly staffed by individuals who were not specifically prepared for their positions. Some very visible individuals in postsecondary education have succeeded without such preparation, and there are some who, even though they had relevant preparation, do not elect to employ their professional counterparts. The attitude of the postsecondary segment of education is particularly troublesome for professors of adult education for several reasons. First, personnel in postsecondary continuing education programs are often colleagues of the professors, and the two groups interact in campus politics. Second, a large majority of students in adult education programs aspire to employment in postsecondary continuing education. Third, the issue relates to professional status.

While hard data are not available to document this observation, it appears that progress is being made in the employment of professionally prepared adult educators in postsecondary continuing education units. We must remember that the history of continuing education units in universities is older than the existence of a professional cadre of educators of adults. It should then come as no surprise that prior to 1965 there was very little opportunity for universities to select people with graduate degrees in adult education for leadership positions. Furthermore, those selected for such positions had no particular commitment to adult education as a field of graduate study. Thus, they often selected subordinates from their own field or on criteria other than educational preparation. Affirmative action requirements and the increasing number of qualified graduates of adult education programs seem to be associated with a trend toward employment of these graduates in postsecondary continuing education units.

Advertisements for administrative personnel in continuing education units of postsecondary institutions now frequently call for degree work in the field. The increasing visibility and acceptance of graduates of adult and continuing education programs focuses attention more directly on the kinds of preparation provided directors of educational programs for adults. Because adult and continuing education is an applied field of study, program directors are expected to possess the management skills appropriate to their institutional function. The next section examines some issues and positions concerning graduate programs of instruction in adult and continuing education.

PROGRAM CONTENT

Since Teachers College at Columbia University awarded the first doctoral degrees in adult education in 1935 to Wilbur C. Hallenbeck and William H. Stacy (Knowles, 1977), a large number of graduate programs in adult education have been created. According to Jain and Carl (1979), 86 institutions offering graduate programs in the field were represented by members of the Commission of Professors of Adult Education of North America in 1979. While it is difficult to obtain a list of all universities that offer a major in adult and continuing education, as of 1981 there were at least 80 such institutions.

The expansion in the number of universities awarding graduate degrees parallels the popular acceptance of the concept of adult and continuing education. Nevertheless, the variety of agencies and institutions providing educational programs and the limited availability of professional adult educators present challenges to graduate programs designed to provide new professionals. For example, the diversities of institutional missions and philosophy complicate the process of "teaching" a specific model of administration and program development.

Earlier in this chapter, we asked what the content of adult and continuing education should be. There is no universal agreement as to the answer, but there are some general areas of consensus.

Aker (1962), Houle (1970), and Liveright (1964) all agree on the importance of research skills for professional competence. One of the themes of this volume relates to the ability of the educator to conduct a special kind of research that informs the program developer of the need for programs in certain areas designed for specific target audiences. While research of this kind may lack some of the trappings of scholarship associated with formal academic research, it requires some of the same skills such as observation, recording of data, analysis and interpretation of findings, and arriving at sound conclusions.

Research that contributes to the origin and development of successful adult and continuing education programs may include a range of distinctive data bases. For example, some program administrators regularly review a variety of journals and magazines to obtain information that may suggest program topics. This process is illustrated by a review I conducted when writing this chapter section. One newspaper article on professional burnout suggested a potential program topic. Two magazine articles addressed such diverse phenomena as "fathering" and microcomputers. The "research" required to fashion any of the above ideas into a successful educational program, however, has only begun with the identification of the topic. The programmer may next place a few telephone calls to colleagues in other parts of the country to obtain additional information concerning the selected topic. Next, a contact may be made with a specialist in the area. If the continuing education programmer is associated with a university, appropriate faculty may contribute useful information. Representatives of the potential audience may also be a source of information. Knowledge of the potential audience will suggest the possibility of a target audience, for example, individuals within certain age, educational, sex, occupational, social role, or income categories. Thus, graduates of programs in adult and continuing education need to be able to use their research skills in the organization and development of program ideas.

Graduate programs in the field seem to cluster in three subject areas: adult psychology, adult education methodology, and the sociology of adulthood. These findings lend credence to White's conclusion (1956) that there is, even among educators in different fields, a common core of training interests. A British educator, K. T. Elsdon (Campbell, 1977, p. 71), has also noted that although there is a range of provision, structure, and content in adult education, the basic staff functions and activities of professional adult educators cut across the differences.

Reputable scholars such as Campbell (1977), Elsdon (1977),

Knox (1979a), and Griffith (1980) fail to agree on the level of una-
nimity of adult educators concerning program content in graduate
study. Yet the evidence seems to support the views of Campbell, Elsdon, and Knox sufficiently to suggest the possibility of modest agreement on broad areas of content including organizations and administration.

ADMINISTRATIVE COMPETENCIES

Houle (1970) identifies administration as one of the four major functions common to educators of adults. Knox (1979a) says there are
three areas of proficiency with special significance for administrators
in adult and continuing education: administration, program development, and the use of research. He further states that administration
includes concern for responsiveness, interpersonal relations, and humanistic values that should provide guidance to professional practice.
Effective administrative practices draw upon research generalizations
from different scholarly disciplines and procedures that contribute to
effectiveness, according to Knox.

Four general components are included in administration (Knox,
1979a). They are as follows: (a) recruitment and retention of learners, (b) acquisition and management of resources, (c) staff recruitment, selection, and development, and (d) leadership that includes
tinuing education programs are potentially subject to a variety of con-
planning and coordination.

RECRUITMENT AND RETENTION OF LEARNERS

Strategies for attracting and retaining students in adult and contemporary developments. Numerous participation and retention
studies have produced an improved understanding of relevant new
factors. These include mandatory continuing education requirements, improved marketing concepts, and a wide range of employer-
sponsored educational programs.

ACQUISITION AND MANAGEMENT OF RESOURCES

Resource acquisition and management constitutes the second administrative function identified by Knox. Both phases of the function
are subject to recent developments. First, administrators of adult and

continuing education programs must compete with administrators of units frequently perceived to be more central to the institutional missions. Such competition for resources becomes more intense when funds are limited. Second, management of financial and physical resources is improved with new electronic data-processing capability. These two developments represent different challenges to the administrator. The first condition is familiar: The experienced program director is accustomed to the challenge of convincing higher-level institutional administrations of the wisdom of increasing support for adult programs. The second development, however, presents the administration with the opportunity to learn how to use the electronic data-processing capability that office microcomputers have made ubiquitous.

STAFF RECRUITMENT, SELECTION, AND DEVELOPMENT

The recruitment, selection, and development of staff is the third important function of adult and continuing education administration. This function is also influenced by current events. Recruitment and selection of staff has become somewhat complicated by efforts to adhere to the letter and spirit of affirmative action and by the increasing population of professionally prepared adult educators. Staff development, according to Knox (1979a), is one of the underdeveloped administrative functions in most university continuing education units.

The staff development procedure is particularly crucial for those employers who persist in hiring individuals with professional experience outside the field of adult and continuing education. The historical precedent for such hiring probably influences current failures to employ professionally prepared staff. Failure to recognize the "socialization" dimensions of graduate preparation, collegial interaction, professional participation, and staff development activities ignores a growing body of literature on this topic.

Ashford (1978), Mezirow, Darkenwald, and Knox (1975), Brady and Long (1972), Everitt (1974), and Farmer (1970) provide convincing information on the importance of graduate preparation, professionalism, and socialization. Assuming that "creativity, imagination, charisma, and strong interpersonal skills" (Cunningham & Veri, 1981, p. 9) are the most important proficiencies needed by programmers in adult and continuing education, how are the philosophical, process, and professional dimensions to be developed? Without strong staff development programs, the practice of employing individuals who do not have the benefits of a graduate experience in adult and continuing education places an organization in jeopardy.

Even among organizations that seek to employ professionally prepared adult educators, the importance of staff development is increasing. The kinds of developments discussed in this volume are of sufficient magnitude to require regular and systematic staff development activities. Staff development procedures themselves can be enhanced and strengthened through the use of the electronic media. To think of staff development only as a group activity is to err. Teleconferences linking several adult and continuing education staffs in various states appear to be an extremely promising use of the new media.

LEADERSHIP

The leadership function is perhaps the most popular of the four functions of administration identified by Knox. Its popularity and visibility is explained by its pervasive impact on all other functional behaviors. Leadership behavior is generally perceived to be an extension of the administration; it is a product of one's experience, education, and philosophy. It reveals much about the individual, and therefore, in many organizations, the administrative activities clearly reflect the imprint of the chief administrative officer.

Leadership style has long been a favorite topic of writers concerned with the issues of personal leadership in organizational units. In the 1960s and 1970s, attention was focused on two polar dimensions of leadership style: the task-oriented style and the person-oriented style. Various studies examined decision-making processes in work units and compared top-down models of autocratic leadership with group decision-making models based on democratic concepts.

Further refinement of research and application of theories of leadership styles led to the Theory X and Theory Y concepts and eventually to the current Theory Z approach. Theory X is basically a task-oriented approach that sees people as generally self-centered, not particularly self-starting, and in need of supervision. In contrast, Theory Y reflects a view of people as other-directed, highly motivated, and able to work with limited supervision. Experienced managers are aware that both Theory X and Theory Y represent an ideal that is seldom achieved in reality. The discrepancy between the ideal X or Y situation is further exacerbated by the lack of universality of work situations. Hence, under certain conditions, Theory X may be more appropriate than others, and so forth. Consequently, a contingency theory has been proposed as a rational means of addressing reality from situation to situation.

Contingency theory is supported by a substantial body of research. Even though Likert (1961) indicates that *most* groups are more productive with a considerate leader, Lawrence and Lorsch (1967) believe that structured departments such as production units seem to be more efficient under authoritarian leaders. In contrast, creative units seem to prosper under considerate leaders. Burns and Stalker (1961) are of the opinion that dynamic organizations respond more positively to a considerate leadership style while stable industries are more successful with authoritarian leaders. It may be concluded (Perrow, 1967) that authoritarian leadership is preferred for tasks that are both structured and routine while considerate leadership is desired for tasks that are both ambiguous and variable.

Theory Z has recently emerged in prominence, at least in part due to the phenomenal success of Japanese businesses in world trade. It has been described as the modification of Japanese management systems to accommodate the needs of American culture. Its components include: (a) a formal philosophy, (b) a long-term focus, (c) emphasis on human qualities, (d) consideration of worker goals, and (e) valuing of employees (Ouchi, 1981).

One of the popular concepts based on Theory Z is the quality circle. Fundamentally, quality circles are an approach to problem solving that brings labor and management together. Through quality circles labor becomes a part of the decision-making process, and people develop a greater pride and interest in their work. Problems considered by a quality circle may include work schedules, tasks, materials, methods, and machinery. Quality circles (a) identify problems, (b) determine their causes, (c) seek the best solutions, and (d) take steps to implement the solutions.

This description of Theory Z shows its relationship to Theory Y, considerate leadership. The Japanese cultural context has provided a more fertile milieu for the new leadership style. Nevertheless, a number of American organizations have implemented Theory Z.

This development has a twofold implication for adult and continuing education. First, Theory Z seems to be an appropriate leadership style in adult and continuing education organizations. Second, it offers attractive program content.

Administrative units of adult and continuing education organizations may reflect a variety of structures. For example, in the complex structure, one person directs numerous subunits, each headed by administrators at a lower level. Some of these subunits may also contain additional divisions with supervisory and management personnel. In contrast, the one-person shop contains only one administrator and clerical/support staff. Relationships between the directors of complex structures and their personnel likely would differ from relationships of directors of one-person units with their staff members. The complex structure appears to contain many of the variables associated with a considerate leadership style, particularly in dynamic areas such as program planning and program development, conference coordination, promotion and publicity, and evaluation. It also contains the possibility for task-oriented styles in certain units such as record keeping, budget management, housekeeping, and related routine activities. Based on the broad outlines of management theory we have discussed, most adult and continuing education units should respond favorably to a person-centered leadership style.

Increasing competition for scarce resources and clients among the growing numbers of adult education providers will place additional emphasis on the administrative skills of program directors. Managers of continuing education organizations will be challenged to provide climates that encourage creative and dynamic approaches to program development. The climate must be sufficiently supportive so that program developers can openly speculate and investigate emerging or predicted trends. They must be supported by equally creative and original thinkers in the marketing and evaluation sections of the organization.

MARKETING ADULT AND CONTINUING EDUCATION

Marketing adult and continuing education is one of the glamour topics in administration today, although prior to 1970 few articles and research reports on publicity and promotion could be found in the field. Some of the more comprehensive treatments of adult and continuing education published earlier reveal the kind of attention previously given to marketing. Brunner et al. (1959) fail to include marketing or promotion in the index of their outstanding work. Less than two pages are devoted to a discussion of promotion of adult and continuing education in the 1960 *Handbook of Adult Education in the United States* (Knowles, 1960). Since the mid-1970s, however, administrators and professors in the field have shown a much greater interest in the topic. It is noteworthy that the interest in marketing closely parallels a decline in the enrollment of college students of traditional age.

Discussions in the 1960 *Handbook of Adult Education in the United States* reveal the thrust and concern of adult and continuing education. Promotion and advertising as discussed in 1960 emphasized creating public understanding and awareness of adult education. The history as reported here, however, fails to reflect fully the activity in the field. Needs-assessment, an important component in marketing, was popular among educators. The use of mailing lists was also studiously observed.

McGee (1959) sheds some light on the attitudes toward marketing among educators. He conducted a survey of "merchandising" practices in adult education that generated strong response against the idea of "selling" this "product." The reaction seems to have been based on two things. First, professional commitment and preoccupation caused educators to believe that they were above the commercial arena. Second, opposition to merchandising adult education may have stemmed from internal pressure groups. McGee notes two such groups. The first is comprised of those who believe that educational institutions should be removed from the larger audience and values of the contemporary culture. The second contains those who believe that there is a huge audience lusting after education; these people think educators have only to provide the structure and content (McGee, 1959).

Between 1965 and 1975, there was a gradual softening of opposition to advertising, merchandising, and promotion of adult education. The Adult Education Association of the United States (Verner & White) published an informative little book in 1965, *Adult Education Theory and Method: Administration of Adult Education*, which contained a reprint of McGee's article and another by Stern

(1965). This publication may be looked on as a kind of watershed, for articles such as those by Wuerger (1971) and Youse (1973) began to appear in the late 1960s and early 1970s.

It was Kotler (Kotler & Levy, 1969) who sparked the interest of educators in marketing. He legitimized marketing as an appropriate activity for all kinds of voluntary organizations. Prior to Kotler's work, many educational institutions were sensitive to the need for sound public relations programs, but these programs did not represent the same kind of emphasis later reflected in marketing activities. According to current concepts, marketing in adult education is perceived as a comprehensive process that includes every phase of an institution's mission and activity with the ultimate purpose of attracting, enrolling, and teaching students.

The marketing concept has been abstracted to reflect four critical elements: product, promotion, price, and place. The integrity of the marketing concept requires appropriate concern and attention to each of the four elements. Service units of educational institutions, however, seem to ignore price as a marketing tool (Buchanan & Barksdale, 1974).

Marketing is more comprehensive than mere promotion, publicity, and needs-assessment. Marketing includes these, but the process goes well beyond traditional activities. Informed by an awareness of the larger social, psychological, and technological developments discussed earlier in this volume, the reader should be able to recognize the significance of marketing as a conceptual and administrative tool in adult and continuing education. We must remember that from 1960 to about 1975, adult and continuing education organizations served generations born before 1945. Those generations are quite different from the largest generation in America's history, which became the potential primary target audience about 1970. The latest target audience, born between 1950 and 1960, will continue to influence educational programming through 1990. Adult and continuing education administrators are challenged to relate their marketing activities to this very market-sophisticated target group, a generation that has been nurtured on some of Madison Avenue's slickest advertising, marketing, and promotional activities.

Administrators must also consider the legal and moral implications of marketing adult and continuing education. There is already evidence that some educators sell their products like traveling medicine shows sold snake oil 100 years ago. Too much "sizzle" in the brochures can easily oversell an educational activity. Failure to deliver on promises made in mail campaigns can greatly undermine the entire area of adult and continuing education for some prospective learners.

Marketing adult and continuing education is likely to become a new career emphasis in the near future. Some administrators of continuing education units are looking to marketing graduates from schools of business and journalism. There is evidence, however, that marketing may also gain a strong position in graduate programs in adult and continuing education, either in the department or as a requirement to be met by marketing courses offered elsewhere.

In the immediate future, organizations will accept the notion of a director of marketing, a marketing department, or the same function by another name where the products and services of the educational unit are marketed. This will not necessarily result in the loss of other administrative positions operating in publications, publicity, and related functions. In one- and two-person shops, however, it may require a shift of emphasis among functions. Administrative functions naturally differ between educational organizations that have large specialized staffs and organizations of the "mom and pop" type.

Data-processing skills and equipment are also likely to be closely related to marketing activities. Electronic computing capability is becoming accessible even to smaller organizations. With proper planning marketing analyses can be greatly facilitated through the use of appropriate skills and electronic data-processing equipment.

OBSTACLES

It is obvious that adult and continuing education practitioners face a variety of obstacles as they attempt to develop successful programs. Adult education graduate programs can go only so far in preparing the administrator to overcome these obstacles. Professors can teach the future administrator the principles of program planning or principles of teaching adults, but if the context of practice rewards the administrator for violating some of these principles, it is not the fault of the program. For example, it is not unusual for program planners to begin by asking Who can we get to be our drawing card? or

Where can we meet? The emphasis is placed immediately on the "resource" step of the planning procedure instead of needs-analysis and also bypasses the question of objectives. Or the motives of participation may be moved from educational ones to entertainment or perhaps the opportunity to visit a new city or golf course. Another example concerns the recruitment of personnel, particularly part-time teachers. In some instances it is obvious that a purpose other than teaching skill has been important in the identification and selection of teachers. Of course, the recruitment and selection of personnel are also influenced by agency or institutional policies that often limit choices.

The need to make money is very real for many adult and continuing education programs. Some university continuing education units must be completely self-supporting while others may receive from 30 to 50 percent of their budgets from the central administration. Administrators of these units are placed in extremely difficult circumstances. They must often choose between a program that is clearly a money-maker and one that is obviously a financial liability. It is noted in chapter 4 that some media programs are based primarily on a "marketing" model rather than a curriculum model.

The images of some programs are regularly besmirched by snide references to "basket-weaving" and "fly-casting" courses, but detractors fail to consider how these "questionable" activities often support other more substantial educational experiences. As long as continuing education is perceived as being a product rather than a service, administrators will find decisions dictated by the need to produce income.

Cunningham and Veri (1981) have also commented on constraints that reduce the potential impact of professionally prepared adult educators in university continuing education organizations. Their conclusions, freely paraphrased and summarized, indicate that conditions of practice are critical factors that limit the effectiveness of graduate adult education programs in developing the desired levels of student proficiency. The negative conditions of practice exist in the graduate programs themselves and also in the units where the practitioner must work.

A similar set of constraints can probably be developed for business and industry, government organizations, volunteer agencies, and other groups. The great diversity of settings and the distinctive missions intrinsic to the various agencies, institutions, and organizations providing adult and continuing education preclude the development of numerous specialized graduate programs. In a few areas such as literacy, community college work, and cooperative extension, the information learned can be transferred to different settings, but even within these popular areas the range of institutional differences is quite wide.

SUMMARY AND CONCLUSIONS

This chapter focused on technological developments in administration and education. Its basic premise implies that a technology of administration of adult and continuing education is required. Based on the literature, there is reason to believe that such a technology is developing (Long, 1983). The published and unpublished comments on the topic often address one or more of five themes: (a) appropriate preparation, (b) the content of adult and continuing education, (c) administrative competencies, (d) marketing, and (e) obstacles to program development. Each of these themes was addressed in the chapter.

The technology of administration and program development in adult and continuing education is admittedly limited. The field has only recently become a profession and a legitimate area of university study. While the education of adults has been an element of most Western cultures for centuries, it tended to remain in the area of the arts and crafts. Since the 1920s, however, the processes of adult and continuing education have received increasing attention, and for almost 50 years American universities have been awarding doctoral degrees for its study.

The parallel growth in adult and continuing education as a field of practice and a field of study focused attention on the development of graduate programs to prepare leaders. In this chapter we have examined the question of who to employ and related topics such as educational program structure and content, leadership, administrative competencies, the marketing of adult and continuing education, and obstacles to program development.

It is beyond question that one of the significant variables in the planning and implementation of adult and continuing education programs is the technology of administration and program development.

IMPLICATIONS

The changes and developments in society discussed in chapters 1 through 4 converge to produce multiple implications for a technology of adult and continuing education. Each of these chapters has shown how the administrator and program developer must possess a set of skills and appropriate knowledge to collect, analyze, synthesize, interpret, and apply a vast array of knowledge about society and electronic (and other) media. In turn, the results of the activity must be translated into programs of learning for adults, or what has been referred to here as a technology of adult and continuing education. Demands to provide such a technology arise from two places. First, graduate programs in the field bear a major responsibility for improving the technology and providing appropriate learning experiences. Second, staff development programs within existing adult and continuing education units must respond to this need.

Special Populations

Overview

As noted in chapter 1, adult and continuing education programs may be classified according to function, program areas, institutions, populations served, and abstract models. In this section we will discuss programs directed toward selected populations or audiences in order to emphasize two points. First, the process of preparing for a selected population is a fruitful one; second, social developments in the past 30 years have influenced programming for some special populations that are generally perceived as having been poorly served in the past. Each population discussed in Part III also may be served by programs designed to satisfy each of the five functions of adult education identified by Bryson (1936) and discussed in chapter 1. Furthermore, programs addressing four of the five functions of adult education are discussed in Part III. Theoretically, the number of populations served by specially designed programs is limited only by the combination of characteristics by which populations can be identified. In Part III we have identified three selected populations: the aging, the disadvantaged, and women.

"Special Populations" focuses on a historical practice in adult and continuing education of developing programs for specific groups. Current procedures used in the origination and development of programs for special populations, however, are much more refined than the shotgun

approach used historically and are the consequence of a
number of developments. First, the development of client-
centered programs indicates that techniques designed to
identify the educational needs and interests of given
groups have been appropriately and successfully employed. Second, social developments have supported philosophical positions that encourage the provision of educational opportunities for special populations such as the
elderly, ethnic and racial groups, the economically disadvantaged, women, and institutionalized persons. Third,
the social conscience that became aware of the need of the
special groups has stimulated associations, foundations,
and governments to fund pilot programs and to provide
additional support.

Each of these three developments is important, but it
is unlikely that individually any would have resulted in
successful programs. The third factor is of course extremely important, for external funding for many of the
programs provided to special populations are likely to be
provided by nonprofit organizations, governmental units,
and public and private not-for-profit educational institutions.

While the three target audiences—the aging, the disadvantaged, and women—are quite dissimilar in many
respects, they all seem to have benefited from a rising
social conscience and sensitivity to issues of educational
equity. The populations are not perceived to be mutually
exclusive; for example, educational programs for the disadvantaged include aged women as well as young men.
Similarly, women's programs and programs for older individuals serve affluent women and disadvantaged women.

In each of the following three chapters, some historical observations are shared and examples of programming
in each area are discussed. The chapter on educational
programs for women also describes recent trends and
problems in light of information obtained from directors
of leading women's programs.

Each chapter in Part III illustrates the dynamic,
creative, pragmatic, pluralistic, and voluntary character-

istics of adult and continuing education. Programming for
each of the populations described reflects an economic, social, and political pragmatism. The histories of each of
the program areas provide a wealth of evidence that supports the thesis of the volume: that programming and the
social context influence each other. As women achieve
greater levels of equality and as the numbers of older
adults increase in American society, the thrusts of programming in these areas are expected to change. It will
be the creative program planners who will benefit first
and foremost from these changes that are already in
progress.

6 Programming for the Aging

As noted in chapter 2, the increasing visibility of older adults, paralleling modifications in the population structure, has contributed to important changes in educational programs for older students. It can be argued that numbers and ratios alone would have been sufficient to sensitize society to the older learner. But it can also be maintained that the contemporary interest in the older adult as a student/learner is part of a larger picture that includes sensitivity to the educational limitations experienced by older individuals and a philosophy supportive of education for the enrichment of adult life. Program planning for aging learners is influenced by the following and related changes:

- Increasing life expectancy is contributing to the expansion of the old old population.
- Increasing improvements in health are expanding the size of the young old population and also contributing to higher activity levels among this demographic group.
- Higher pensions and related economic developments have resulted in an expanding number of relatively affluent aging individuals.
- Educational achievement levels are rising among aging Americans.

✝ Designing and offering programs for the aging is a particular challenge to adult educators. First, as illustrated in the following pages, adult educators believe that older adults need to participate in educational activities. Second, although the increasing number of aging Americans represents an attractive population for adult education, their participation rates have historically been lower than those of middle-aged and young adults. To translate into action the belief that older adults are a desirable population for adult and continuing education, educators must resolve two problems: designing and providing programs for the aging and obtaining their participation.

Support for educational opportunity for adults is a phenomenon not much older than 20 years. McClusky (1978) believes that prior to the 1971 White House Conference on Aging, there was very little interest or activity in the education of older adults. Since 1971, however, both the priority accorded the needs of older adults and educational opportunity for them have increased.

Adult educators and educational gerontologists have been casting about for at least two decades in order to improve program attractiveness. Some, such as Hendrickson and Barnes, maintain that education for older students should be designed principally as a tool for problem solving. Accordingly, they make the following comment: "Older persons as a group tend to be faced with numerous personal and social problems without adequate resources to meet them" (1967, p. 3). Londoner (1971) agrees that aging adults need strategies or education designed to help them cope with challenges posed by a dynamic society. He believes that the older adult must develop and strengthen personal competencies to face the challenges of old age. Others argue for redesign of the educational system. Hiemstra (1973) supplements the foregoing views with his observation that adult educators must regard the aged as clientele with special needs and interests.

Peterson (1976) has cogently addressed both parts of the challenge: program development and recruitment. He contends that despite increased interest in the older adult as a learner, many older people feel that education has no relevance to their lives. After comparing their interest in education with other interests, he observed that older people just do not feel a need for education.

The current popularity of educational programs for the aging is not yet universal, and at this writing, stresses in the American economy threaten recent progress. Assuming that economic and political pressures to dismantle much of the program area that includes education for older adults are successfully resisted, the current range, variety, and quality of educational opportunities for the aging are likely to increase. Therefore, with an optimistic eye to the future, this chapter is designed to (a) examine concepts and philosophy in the provision of education for the aging, (b) discuss adult ability, (c) briefly trace the development of educational programming for aging Americans in the 1970s, (d) describe justifications for participation, and (e) identify and describe some of the programs that exist for older adults.

CONCEPTS AND PHILOSOPHY

Education for aging individuals is characterized by a plethora of concepts and justifications that have program implications. First, some gerontologists prefer to use the term *education for the aging* as a substitute for other less desirable terms such as *senior citizens, elderly,* and *older-aged.* Others prefer conceptually based definitions. Peterson (1976) cites three such definitions for educational gerontology: (a) education for older learners, (b) education of general or specific publics about older people, and (c) preparation within the formal definition of higher education. The third category includes professional or liberal education of persons at a postsecondary level, whether for preservice or continuing education, concerning gerontological issues.

The philosophical orientations in education for aging are evident in four distinct models (Moody, 1978). The first model is based on the philosophy of rejection, an idea that involves avoidance, repression, neglect, isolation, and expendability; it provides no rationale for educating older adults. The philosophical arguments that support this model include views of the old as nonproductive, parasitic, and weakened competitors for scarce goods and resources. This view is shown in the novel *Centennial* (Michener, 1974) when Blue Leaf, the Indian woman, is left to starve and freeze after the death of her husband, Lame Beaver. It is regrettable that this primitive concept of rejection of the value of aging individuals continues to persist in contemporary society. The second model is subscribed to by liberal, political activists and proponents of the welfare state; it is a social services model. In this view educational opportunity for the aging is a form of entertainment that keeps them busy and frequently reduces the pressure for other more expensive services.

The third model is based on the concept of activity; its adherents believe that life continues to be valued among the aging and that evidence of the value of life is at least in part related to activity. Thus, education is designed to introduce older people to, and maintain them in, leadership development, preparation for second careers, and other activities purposefully designed to keep them in the mainstream of life. The fourth model extends the third and is presented as self-actualization. Herein human life is represented as having an unending potential for development. Maturity is seen as an unusual time for achievements that are built upon earlier life periods. This view, perhaps more than the others, romanticizes later life. The goal of the September period is visualized as an objective psychological development across the life-span, and education is perceived as an appropriate element in the attainment of the highest psychological goal of fulfillment in the last stage of the human ethic.

Other models exist, but they seem to be redundant or extensions of one of these four philosophical orientations. The models thus can be placed on a continuum that positions the barbaric concept of expendability at one extreme and the transcendental concept that places great reverence on life at any stage, but which especially values the aging, at the other end. Political, economic, and social dimensions of the culture are closely allied with one or more of these four basic models.

ADULT ABILITY

Administrators and others concerned with the development of adult and continuing education programs are supported by an extensive body of literature concerning the ability of adults. For more than a century, scholars have been accumulating data concerning the physical and cognitive abilities of adults at different ages across the life-span. Research has found increasing expectations and continuously rising performance levels at later ages. As this topic is more extensively developed in chapter 3, no further comment is required here. The research is noted primarily to remind us that education programs for adults are often discussed within a framework that includes questions regarding the abilities of aging individuals. In most instances data today indicate that the question of adult ability, at least through the seventh decade of life, has become a moot point.

DEVELOPMENT OF PROGRAMS FOR THE AGING

Programs designed especially for aging learners arose in the late 1940s and in the 1950s. The three early White House Conferences on Aging, held in 1950, 1961, and 1971, present sound evidence of the concern for the special needs of the aging. The Older Americans Act is cited by Stanford (1978) as the first definite base of funding for the field of gerontology. Furthermore, he credits the legislation with validating programs in gerontology in educational institutions. Shortly after the Administration on Aging began operation, a personnel survey entitled *Manpower Needs in the Field of Aging* (1968) was conducted. As a result the training of practitioners and teachers in applied gerontology was among the early priorities of the Administration on Aging. The administration's general priorities were to prepare practitioners for state and federal planning and administration, community programs, management and administration of retirement housing and homes for the aged, and direction of multipurpose senior citizens' centers serving older people through adult education, architectural design, counseling, library services, recreation, and other fields (Stanford, 1978).

Since the late 1960s, education for older adults has grown into one of the most dynamic areas in education and gerontology (McClusky, 1978). McClusky believes that education for older adults has two functions: increasing "copeability" and achieving fulfillment. The coping area should focus first on adult basic education, according to McClusky, for three reasons: (a) research indicates that older adults have less formal education than any other age group, (b) a minimum standard of competence in reading, writing, and computation is a basic prerequisite for participation in American society, and (c) instruction in basic educational skills, such as reading, writing, and arithmetic, is a recognized task of education.

A second and broader component of the "copeability" function consists of education that is primarily designed to help the elderly face the challenge of daily life in a dynamic society. The area includes instruction for the prevention of illness and promotion of health, political economics, transportation, estate planning, and the use of leisure.

The broadest and most diverse educational dimension for older individuals, according to McClusky (1978), is the area of personal fulfillment. This area contains at least four subcategories of instructional and learning activity: (a) the expressive, (b) the contributive, (c) the influencing, and (d) the transcendent.

Thorson (1978, pp. 218–22) has offered the following list of learning tasks for older adults:

1. Adapting to change
2. Continuing to grow
3. Perpetuating the culture
4. Putting one's life into perspective
5. Finding self-acceptance
6. Remaining integrated in society
7. Maintaining control and avoiding helplessness

There are natural overlaps between the lists of McClusky and Thorson. While these are just two of many different formulations of learning tasks or activities proposed for older adults, they serve well to illustrate areas of difference and agreement.

Hiemstra (1972) surveyed 86 aging adults in a study designed to determine what types of education and locations for instruction were preferred. He found that his sample favored instrumental educational activities conducted in senior citizens' centers. He also sought to identify some of the obstacles to participation. His subjects provided the following list, ranked in order of importance (p. 106):

1. Transportation problems
2. Don't like to go out at night
3. Can learn by self
4. Courses not interesting
5. Courses cost too much
6. Too much time involved
7. Miscellaneous

No current inventory of educational opportunities for the aging is available, but it is safe to assume that the magnitude of programs discovered by DeCrow (1974) continues to exist. He reported that the majority of the 3,500 educational delivery agencies he queried reported the introduction of new programs for older adults in the year preceding the survey. At least one-half of those surveyed also shared plans to *add* new programs during the following year.

JUSTIFICATIONS FOR PARTICIPATION

As noted earlier, society reflects at least four philosophical justifications for education for the aging. We also observed that McClusky's two large classifications of educational functions (1978) can be sub-divided into at least six subfunctions. The subcategories of copeabil-ity are adult basic education and problems of daily living, and the subcategories of personal fulfillment are (a) the expressive, (b) the contributive, (c) the influencing, and (d) the transcendent. Others (Hiemstra, 1972; Marcus, 1977; and Riddell, 1976) have studied the participation interests of older individuals.

Havighurst's construct of expressive and instrumental objectives of education has been attractive to investigators studying motivation of older adults for educational participation. A brief description of the two types of education by function, as identified by Havighurst, is as follows:

> Instrumental education means education for a goal which lies outside and beyond the act of education. In this form, education is an instrument for changing the learner's situation. . . . Instru-mental education is thus a kind of investment of time and energy in the expectation of future gain. . . .
>
> Expressive education means education for a goal which lies within the act of learning, or is so closely related to it that the act of learning appears to be the goal. . . . Expressive educa-tion is a kind of consumption of time and energy for present gain. (1964, pp. 17–18)

Prior to Marcus's work (1977), there was a strong belief that older adults preferred expressive educational opportunities even though survey data revealed higher participation among the young old, those less than 60, in job-related courses and programs. Londoner (1971) took issue with the position. He concludes that educational needs of older adults focus on activities with instrumental value. Marcus (1977) may have helped unravel some of the confusion: He found that with age, perception of which is more useful—instrumen-tal or expressive education—tends to shift. According to Marcus, this shift occurs although competent judges may perceive the activities participated in as instrumental. These findings suggest the complex-ity of the program developer's task in adult and continuing educa-tion. Developers must provide programs that address learning needs of older adults that require instrumental activities/topics for fulfill-ment while the prospective learner tends to perceive that educational event as satisfying an expressive need.

Additional evidence of the difficulty of defining an educational activity as instrumental or expressive is provided by Whatley

(1974). At least three important potential conclusions can be derived from Whatley's findings: (a) professionals had projected their values and as a result selected a higher percentage of instrumental educational topics, (b) older adults do prefer instrumental topics, and (c) because attribution of instrumental/expressive characteristics is a highly idiosyncratic act, it is difficult to determine how individuals perceive a given activity or topic.

Participation of older adults in educational programs is favored by those whose philosophical position includes models two, three, and four, identified early in this discussion. It is perceived to be a positive adaptive response to the challenges faced by aging individuals approaching retirement (Pritchard, 1978). Through educational activities the older adult meets needs identified by McClusky (1978) or, as noted by Pritchard (1978), develops increased social competence to deal with personal changes and losses associated with employment status, health, and social relationships while also coping with consumer and environmental challenges and rapid technological and social developments.

Despite the benefits attributed to educational participation by adult educators and educational gerontologists, rates of participation frequently have been disappointingly low. National surveys have consistently revealed that a decline in participation is apparent after age 50 and extremely conspicuous after age 60. Depending upon the research definition, only 4 to 9 percent of people over age 55 participate in formal educational programs (Johnstone & Rivera, 1965; National Center for Education Statistics, 1980).

Despite voluminous research concerning reasons for participation in adult education, little effort has been expended on comparative studies of motivation patterns, needs-assessments, and other characteristics between adults of different age groups. Survey work generally has been based on instruments, research justifications, and heuristic theories developed for all adults. Furthermore, the design of these studies has often provided cross-sectional data on extremely small samples. Even though the survey instrument was superficially revised for an older population, Riddell's study (1976), for example, used a small sample of 84. Morstain and Smart's (1974) study involved 648 people, but it was not designed specifically for an older adult population and did not provide comparative data on motives of young and older adults.

If one can assume the validity of Erikson's (1963) two main late adult stages—generativity versus stagnation and ego integrity versus despair—and/or the validity of Havighurst's (1964) and Maslow's (1962) formulations concerning developmental tasks and self-actualization, the function of education and motivation for participation must differ for 25-year-olds and 55-year-olds.

Survey data show that learning through individual tutoring and participation in community agency-sponsored programs is relatively highest among those over 60. This suggests the possibility of different motivations for education and perceptions of its function. The relative importance of noncredit educational activities is also much higher among older than younger adults. While such an observation may be commonplace, these factors along with other characteristics of older adults' participation preferences in educational activities, may contribute to an analytical framework more productive than the casual acceptance of low participation rates as an unchangeable fact or the belief that participation of older adults is adequately explained and described by existing studies.

DISTINCTIVE PROGRAM CONCEPTS

There is such a variety of program concepts in education for the aging that a chapter can provide only a few illustrations. The references and illustrative programs discussed here, however, should prove useful to both the practicing professional and the apprentice-learner.

TUITION WAIVER PROGRAMS

One of the more nontraditional program concepts concerning education for the aging in the early 1970s was the tuition waiver program, designed to reduce or eliminate tuition fees for older students at public and private postsecondary institutions. The concept, which took many forms among the various states and institutions involved, was based on the premise that people of retirement age should receive free tuition in recognition of taxes paid over their working lives.

Butcher (1980), Florio (1978), Long (1980a), and Long and

Rossing (1978) conducted several national surveys to determine the growth and development of tuition waivers across the nation. Their combined research found that provisions are available either in private or public postsecondary schools in at least 43 states. They agree that the response to the tuition waiver opportunity has been very uneven across the country and even within states. Most institutions responding to Butcher's (1980) survey reported zero to 99 students enrolled in credit and noncredit courses. Approximately half of all reporting community colleges annually enrolled fewer than 100 older students in credit courses under the tuition waiver privilege, and about one-fourth enrolled fewer than 100 in noncredit programs.

Long (1980a) and Long and Rossing (1978) studied the characteristics of tuition waiver programs in state university systems. They found that attitudes among administrators vary but are generally favorable. Respondents saw more benefits than drawbacks associated with the system. Most administrators believe the tuition waiver program benefits the institution and all participants including younger sudents, who have an opportunity to interact with students aged 60 to 75. In the few instances where performance data were reported, the older students as a group maintained higher grade point averages, except when compared with graduate students.

State tuition waiver programs for the elderly are required or permitted by legislatures and by central coordinating agency policy. Table 6.1 reports the provisions of legislative and constitutional action in 19 states, and table 6.2 reports provisions of coordinating board policy in 8 states.

The statutes enacted by various legislatures are not uniform from state to state in the form, provisions, conditions, and criteria which they address or establish. As table 6.1 shows, in most states enabling acts are a product of the legislature. Georgia citizens, however, resorted to a constitutional amendment to authorize tuition waivers. In California the legislature passed a two-year pilot project to test the tuition waiver approach at two state universities. Laws in the other 17 states generally cover public higher education institutions, but technical schools in 6 states were specifically included in the scope of these laws. Some state laws grant higher education institutions the authority to waive or reduce tuition for senior citizens but do not require such a practice. Others require tuition waivers, and some are not clear on this point. California, Hawaii, and Wash-

TABLE 6.1: Legislative or Constitutional Provisions Regarding Senior Citizen Tuition Waivers

State	Year Passed	Minimum Age	Residence Requirement	Space Available Only	Eligible for Credit	Extent of Tuition Waiver
Arkansas	1975[a]	60	No	Yes	Yes	Full
California	1975[b]	60	Yes	Yes	Yes	Full
Connecticut	—[c]	62	No	Yes[d]	Yes	Full
Georgia	1976[e]	62	Yes	Yes	Yes	Full
Hawaii	1974	60	Yes	Yes	Yes	Full
Kentucky	1976	65	Yes	Yes	Yes	Full
Louisiana	1975	65	No	No	Yes	Full
Minnesota	1975	62	Yes	Yes	Yes	$2/Credit Hr.
Montana	1974	62	Yes	No	Yes	Full
New York	1974	60	No	Yes	Audit Only	Full
North Carolina	1975	65	Yes	Yes	Yes	Full
Ohio	1976	60	Yes	Yes	Audit Only	Full
Rhode Island	1976	65	Yes	Yes	Yes	Full
South Carolina	1974	65	Yes	Yes	Yes	Full
Tennessee	1974[a]	65[f]	No	No	Yes[f]	Special Fee
Texas	1975	65	No	Yes	Audit Only	Full
Utah	1977	62	Yes	Yes	Yes	Special Fee
Virginia	1974[a]	60	Yes	Yes	Yes	Full
Washington	1975	60	Yes	Yes	Yes	Partial[g]

Provision		Minimum Age	Residence Requirement	Space Available Only	Eligible for Credit	Extent of Tuition Waiver
		60 62 65	Yes No	Yes No	Yes No	Full Part. Fee Spec. Fee
Total		7 5 7	13 6	16 3	16 3	15 2 2

Note: From H. B. Long & B. E. Rossing, Tuition waivers for older Americans, *Lifelong Learning: The Adult Years*, 1978, *1* (10), 11. Reprinted with permission.

[a] Amended in 1977.
[b] Two-year pilot project at two state universities only.
[c] Date of legislation not available for Connecticut.
[d] Connecticut—first come, first served if accepted in degree program.
[e] Georgia—constitutional amendment.
[f] Tennessee—Sixty-year-olds receive tuition waiver for audited courses.
[g] Washington—Some institutions have full waiver; some have partial waiver.

ington prohibit institutions from establishing additional classes or special classes for senior citizens under the provisions of the special legislation.

Certain provisions are addressed specifically by most if not all laws. Table 6.1 shows the provisions of acts in each state concerning minimum age, residence requirements, registration priority, extent of waivers, and eligibility for credit in free courses. A review of the table shows that the minimum age for receiving a senior citizen tuition waiver varies from age 60 to 65 across the 19 states. Two of every 3 states impose a residence requirement on those wishing to take free courses. Nearly all of the states require those requesting a waiver of tuition to register on a space-available basis. In most states statutes allow a full waiver of tuition. Some states also waive other incidental admission and student fees. Two states authorize partial reduction of tuition, and two others authorize setting a separate special fee for senior citizens.

Finally, it should be noted that two states impose additional conditions on senior citizens applying for tuition waiver benefits. The annual income of senior citizens in Virginia must not exceed $5,000 if they elect to seek credit in a course without paying tuition. Senior citizens taking coursework for a salary increase or to upgrade credentials are not eligible for a tuition waiver in the state of Washington. These two states also limit the number of courses that an individual may take at one time under the tuition waiver provisions. Washington citizens may take only two courses per term, and Virginia residents are limited to three.

In eight states a state-system higher education board as defined by Long and Rossing (1978) has authorized tuition waiver entitlements for senior citizens attending member institutions. Policy statements adopted by these higher education boards address the same elements as the state laws reviewed in table 6.1. Table 6.2 displays the policy provisions concerning the basic conditions and criteria reviewed under the state laws. The minimum age required by governing boards is slightly higher than those of state laws. Seven of eight state boards set the minimum age at 62 or 65. In contrast to the state laws, only two of the eight policy statements specifically establish a state residence requirement for persons requesting tuition waivers. Five of the eight higher education boards require senior citizens using the tuition waiver benefit to register on a space-

TABLE 6.2: Policy Statement Provisions Regarding Senior Citizen Tuition Waivers

State	Year Passed	Minimum Age			Residence Requirement		Space Available Only		Eligible for Credit		Extent of Tuition Waiver
		60	62	65	Yes	No	Yes	No	Yes	No	
Idaho	1974	60				No	Yes		Yes		$5/Course
Kansas	1974			65		No	Yes		Yes		Full
Nevada	—[a]		62			No		No	Yes		Full
North Dakota	1975			65		No	Yes			Audit Only	Full
Oregon	1976			65		No	Yes			Audit Only	Full
South Dakota	1974			65		No	Yes		Yes		¼ Tuition
Vermont	1975		62		Yes			No	Yes		Full
Wisconsin	1974		62		Yes			No		Audit Only	Full
		60	62	65	Yes	No	Yes	No	Yes	No	Full Part. Spec. Fee Fee
Provision Total		1	3	4	2	6	5	3	5	3	6 2 0

Note: From H. B. Long & B. E. Rossing, Tuition waivers for older Americans, Lifelong Learning: The Adult Years, 1978, 1 (10), 12. Reprinted with permission.
[a] Nevada—date of policy not available.

available basis. This is a somewhat lower percentage than that found among state laws. Also, the percentage of board tuition waiver policies that restrict senior citizens to auditing (38 percent) is greater than the comparable percentage of state laws (17 percent). Most board policies provide a full waiver of tuition as do most state laws. Two state higher education boards provide for a reduced tuition charge.

Policy statements of most higher education boards do not always clearly indicate whether noncredit adult education classes as well as regular credit courses are covered. Nevada's policy states that the full tuition waiver applies only to regular institutionally supported courses. Senior citizens receive a waiver of half the registration fee if they enroll in self-sustaining courses (summer session, off-campus, continuing education, community service), provided the course is otherwise self-sustaining. Boards in the other seven states do not mention the application of tuition waiver benefits to noncredit or self-sustaining courses. North Dakota, however, does restrict the tuition waiver program to on-campus courses.

Only two state higher education boards have established additional conditions beyond those just described. In Vermont senior citizens applying for the benefit must be retired or, if employed, must not be employed full time. Wisconsin limits enrollment to two courses per semester.

Examination of the provisions of state laws and state-system higher education–board policy statements shows a basic pattern with some state-to-state variations. Tuition waiver policies grant senior citizens a full waiver of tuition when they enroll in regular credit courses on a space-available basis. The minimum age varies from 60 to 65. The senior citizens may register for credit or audit the courses they take under these provisions. In a few states, they are limited to auditing courses or to partial tuition reductions. Other variations allow the elderly to register on a first-come, first-served basis and to take noncredit and self-sustaining courses without payment of tuition. In comparison to these state laws, state system policies tend to set slightly higher minimum age requirements and are more likely to restrict senior citizens to course auditing.

When learning activities were ranked according to frequency of eligibility for tuition waiver provisions, the following list emerged:

1. Day credit classes
2. Evening credit classes

3. Credit off-campus classes
4. Correspondence
5. Noncredit short courses
6. Noncredit conferences   (Long, 1980a, p. 143)

Even after 10 years, during which time hundreds of U.S. post-secondary educational institutions adopted tuition waiver plans for senior citizens, embarrassingly little is known about the diverse programs scattered among 43 states (Florio, 1978; Long & Rossing, 1978; Miller, 1975). The new world of educational access for mature adults remains virtually unknown. A few studies such as those just cited report some of the basic outlines of the tuition waiver idea. The Academy for Educational Development (1974) estimates that legislative action has reduced tuition charges for adults at nearly 700 colleges and suggests that one-fourth of all colleges and universities in the United States have either dropped or drastically reduced tuition charges for senior adults. Such a development, coupled with demographic projections that suggest an increasing number of senior adults in the population over the next half-century, contains significant implications for U.S. postsecondary education (Long, 1980a).

INSTITUTE FOR LEARNING IN RETIREMENT

Duke University's Institute for Learning in Retirement has taken a different approach from the tuition waiver program. While the cost of enrollment has been kept at a minimum (in 1977 it was $8 per month, or $96 annually), the emphasis is on "peer" relationships. The peer idea includes several components according to Lefstein and O'Barr (1978). It recognizes (a) the difference between older learners and regular students, (b) the range of differences that may characterize an older adult sample, and (c) the input that adult learners may make to the development and design of an adult learning activity.

Peer teaching takes on several characteristics depending upon the skills of the students and the learning content. In one reported course, "A Trip Through the Light Fantastic," one of the institute members, a retired physics professor, explained the physical properties of light to several learners who were also members. Mutual membership in the institute in a sense made them peers, according to Lefstein and O'Barr (1978), but they also observe that the group clearly fell into the traditional classroom instruction pattern.

In other instances institute members may share a similar interest and level of knowledge. One group, for example, expressed an interest in a comparative study of religions but possessed no acknowledged expert to act in the traditional teacher role. A member volunteered to serve as the group coordinator; seeking advice from professionals in the community, he developed a rough course outline, prepared a bibliography, and placed appropriate reading material on reserve in the university library. The coordinator then chaired the first meeting of the class when members collectively determined their objectives for the following 10 sessions.

In addition to the peer teaching practices developed at the institute, activities are frequently coordinated with other special program areas, such as a summer Elderhostel program, and there is also cooperation with the North Carolina Humanities Committee.

It is noteworthy that whereas the institute concept tends to segregate the older learners from the mass of young students of traditional age, there is a healthy interaction between the young and old. The interaction appears to be on a kind of self-selecting basis where young students initiate a contact with a special institute member or vice versa; it is not then unusual for the young student to have increasing contact with a number of institute members.

The Bridge at Bellingham

A third program concept, one that provides intergenerational contact, is the bridge project at the Western Washington University in Bellingham (Rich, 1978). The project is located at Fairhaven College, a cluster campus of 500 students within the larger university. A walkway, referred to as the "bridge," connects a preschool playground with apartment buildings housing students aged 55 and over. The walkway thus provides a physical link between members of the college community from age 2 to 82. Rich (1978) describes a scene that at a given moment might include young children playing in a courtyard traversed by a young adult couple on their way to class and an older student conversing with a young adult student. The bridge concept was originally developed as a means of educational enrichment for the traditional college-age student, but it soon became evident that all three generations gained equally from the project. Therefore, the program recently has been specifically oriented to structure a mix of age groups in a natural way. It now brings together programs involving four groups: (a) a day care center for 40 preschool children of university students, (b) the Bellingham Cooperative School for 40 children, aged 5 to 11, (c) 400 students ranging in age from the late teens to the late forties, and (d) 40 older adult students, most of whom live on campus, attend regular classes, and are involved in extracurricular activities.

ELDERHOSTEL

The Elderhostel concept reveals the dynamic dimensions of programming for individuals over 60. Elderhostel came into being in 1975 at five New Hampshire colleges and universities under the sponsorship of the University of New Hampshire. Writing in the *Midwest Motorist,* Sitek (1980, p. 7) said, "Elderhostel has swept across the nation's college campuses like wildfire and its growing popularity insures that the fire will burn even brighter in the future." In 1975 the five New Hampshire schools offered 15 weeks of programs and enrolled 220 participants. In 1976, 69 weeks of programs were offered at 21 colleges in six New England states. Enough applicants were turned away to fill an additional 2,000 rooms. In 1980, 330 colleges representing all 50 states and Canada offered 670 program weeks and provided 20,000 accommodations. By 1983 the Elderhostel organization expects to enroll 50,000 individuals.

Marty Knowlton, the creator of Elderhostel, was quoted as saying, "The single most pervasive need of older people in the United States is not food, clothing, or shelter, but it is the need for a sense of significant self. Their lives must show significance" (Sitek, 1980, p. 8). It appears that the Elderhostel concept has focused on this important need programmatically and conceptually.

According to Sitek (1980), Elderhostel is an independent, nonprofit organization designed to serve older adults. It responds to their capacity to meet change and intellectual challenge by nourishing a spirit of adventure. Elderhostel coordinates a nationwide network of short-term residential educational experiences for individuals 60 and older. Participating institutions include colleges and universities, independent schools, and specialized study and conference centers.

The Elderhostel program includes materials in the sciences and the liberal and fine arts. There are no entrance requirements, and admission is not based on any academic credential. Participants have ranged from high school dropouts to people with doctorates and represent a broad spectrum of occupational backgrounds. Since Elderhostel does not grant credit, individuals often choose their courses based on a lifetime interest rather than an experiment in formal study. Participants bring to the classroom a kind of excitement and curiosity that is unusual in formal education today, according to several Elderhostel instructors.

Typically, Elderhostels are one week long, beginning on a Sunday evening and ending the following Saturday morning. Participants can elect to take one, two, or all three courses offered daily by regular members of the institution's faculty. The courses deliberately avoid any age-specific courses such as a focus on problems of the elderly. Within the limits of the program format, each Elderhostel institution is encouraged to create an educational experience that is distinctive, calling on the academic strengths of the institution and the unique extracurricular and social environment that characterize the campus community. The Elderhostelers live in dormitories, eat in cafeterias, and attend concerts, plays, debates, exhibits, and lectures. The spirit is a positive one consistent with the tradition of hosteling, of looking for new and interesting elements of the experience and not expecting facilities or service in any way equal to what is available commercially.

At each institution a campus director selects the faculty, solicits the courses for each program week, and makes the logistical arrangements necessary to accommodate each group of participants. In each state one of the institutions coordinates the schedule of program weeks, recruits new institutions to the program, ensures a high standard of quality, promotes the program on a statewide basis, and in general serves as the Elderhostel spokesman in the area.

In 1979, 80 percent of the participants were retired. Twenty-nine percent had graduate degrees, and 1 percent possessed only an elementary education. Other educational achievement distributions were: high school, 12 percent; some college, 27 percent; college degree, 16 percent; some graduate school, 15 percent. The income distribution among participants in 1979 was as follows: under $6,000, 15 percent; $6,000–$12,000, 40 percent; $12,000–$20,000, 26 percent; $20,000–$30,000, 14 percent; over $30,000, 5 percent (Sitek, 1980).

Participants in the Elderhostel program also come from a variety of career backgrounds. In 1979, 50 percent were from a professional field, 11 percent from managerial and administrative fields, 14 percent from a clerical background, and 1 percent had done physical labor, including farm work.

Since its founding, Elderhostel has required that each of its participating institutions be able to host its program using as income a single maximum national tuition. In 1978 the all-inclusive weekly tuition was $105 per person. In 1979 the figure rose to $115, of which $15 served as an administrative allocation in support of Elderhostel state and national offices. The $100 balance was available directly to the college or university for program support.

The issue of tuition is a sensitive one within the Elderhostel family. The extremely low tuition represents a strong commitment to make the program accessible to the broadest possible spectrum of the older population. On the other hand, participating institutions have to be assured that they will not lose money in sponsoring the program. In 1979 Elderhostel aggressively pursued three policies designed to provide financial stability for its campus program without compromising its commitment to maximum accessibility.

First, the Supplemental Tuition Fund was established to provide additional increments of funding to programs with marginal enrollment. The fund was not intended to remove the risk of low enrollments at specific institutions but can be considered a capital investment in support of new programs. As such, the fund was particularly helpful to first-year programs that had attracted 10 to 15 registrants but would have had to have been cancelled because tuition income would not offset program cost. Supplemental tuition increments to averaged fixed costs were negotiated, and with this additional support the institutions agreed to proceed with the program. In all, over $5,500 was converted from this fund in support of 31 weeks of programs in 1979. Second, using the new centralized national registration system, a concerted effort was made to register individuals in underenrolled programs, provided that programs of their first choice were filled. The result was an increase in the average weekly enrollment throughout the Elderhostel network from 27 to 29. It is hoped that participating institutions of proven quality and appeal will be able to count on enrollments of at least 30 persons, the amount Elderhostel recommends to institutions to achieve their break-even budgets (Sitek, 1980).

Finally, Elderhostel established on a trial basis a national hosteling fund to assist individuals who wish to attend Elderhostels but whose income is inadequate to cover even its modest tuition. A simple procedure was designed to determine need, and all those receiving the national catalogue were invited to apply if they required this kind of additional support. Over 50 individuals were granted such support, which totaled over $2,300 in 1979 (Sitek, 1980).

PRERETIREMENT EDUCATION

Preretirement programs were among the first educational programs specifically designed for older adults. Baker (1952) and Tuckman and Lorge (1952) provide some early insights into the challenge of developing appropriate and useful preretirement educational experiences. The programs vary, but there are some common elements such as counseling efforts to ease the transition from active worker to retired worker and financial planning, including explanations of pension plans and Social Security and insurance provisions.

Preretirement educational programs thus have a psychological dimension and a financial dimension. The psychological dimension also includes issues concerning continued "involvement" in society, disengagement issues, attitudes toward retirement, and identification of other interests to replace those of the workplace. The financial dimension is basically concerned with those issues related to maintaining an acceptable quality of life through wise use of retirement resources.

Seltzer has identified three factors that are directly related to successful preretirement education programs: (a) good and pertinent course materials, (b) field experiences that permit the direct exposure of participants to older people, under supervised conditions, and (c) enthusiastic, dedicated, and competent teachers (Seltzer, 1977).

It can be argued that the sum and substance of preretirement education has been effective. Preretirement education programs, however, can successfully address a range of cognitive or informational topics with limited impact on the participant. This limited impact is a result of attitudinal considerations. For example, can one's negative concept of retirement and aging be changed by a better understanding of retirement living centers, Social Security, or health insurance? It is equally important to alter significantly stereotypes and debilitating attitudes held by older people about themselves and the future.

Success, however, will be limited in this area without some basic changes in the socialization processes and media reports that contribute to the development of values.

SUMMARY AND CONCLUSIONS

This chapter discusses five topics concerning adult education programming. It is suggested that each of the subjects examined reflects in some way broader sociological, psychological, and technological changes occurring in American society. The topics addressed are: (a) concepts and philosophical positions concerning education for older people, (b) research about the ability of older adults to learn, (c) development of educational programming for aging Americans, (d) justifications or reasons for participation, and (e) five specific kinds of educational provisions for older adults.

Official concern for educational opportunities for older Americans, as reflected in governmental policies, is of recent origin. McClusky (1978), one of the leaders in the field, suggests that the concern can be traced to the late 1960s. Rudimentary foundations may be stretched backward to the years immediately following World War II.

The contemporary concern is directly associated with significant alterations in American society that resulted from events of the 1940s. Demography, technology, economics, and philosophy, as reflected in attitudes toward self, work, and society, interacted in the ferment of American society in the 1960s in such a manner that the increasing elderly proportion of the American population was accorded greater personal worth and dignity. The consequent recognition of older Americans as valued individuals logically led to the provision of services consistent with such an image. The provision of educational opportunities is also associated with such developments as work benefits offering earlier retirement and better financial security. At the same time, the average life-span of both men and women was increasing. Hence, individuals who retire between 60 and 65 often can look forward to 15 to 20 years of retirement life. The development provided a justification for attainment of some goals that were deferred at an earlier stage of life. Educational activities are sometimes included in those goals.

In spite of the newness of the idea that lifelong learning really does include older people, its popular acceptance and support have been encouraging. Mixed data lead to varying interpretations of the "success" of programs in attracting older citizens. While the percentage of individuals above age 55 annually engaged in learning activities is extremely low, adults in this older age category increased their rate of participation in the 1970s.

IMPLICATIONS

The future is not clear, however. At this writing, the effect of federal changes in Social Security, elevated minimum retirement ages, the loosening of mandatory retirement laws, and severe inflation may have negative effects on programming for older Americans. At best, the changes previously discussed, along with others such as group living patterns for older people and the visibility of the old as targets of crime and heavy consumers of medical care, encourage adult and continuing educators to be creative in future programming activities. Preferences of older people for learning activities conducted during the daylight hours and at locations that do not require much travel time or expenditure of energy are other variables that seem to have implications for programming for the group aged 55 and older.

Knowledge creation also poses implications for educational programs for older Americans. Although the myth of limited ability to learn at advanced ages has been disproven, knowledge advances strongly affect the elderly for several reasons: (a) the new knowledge frequently requires an adaptive response in areas of lifelong practice, (b) new learning must take place at a time when incentives for learning and changing life-styles are weaker, and (c) new knowledge must be obtained at a time when other life responsibilities may make heavy alternative demands.

The programs reviewed in this chapter show that innovative educational programming for older adults is possible. Applications of electronic media in programs for older Americans, however, are not very evident in the literature. The electronic media contain promise for addressing a number of problems such as scheduling programs during daylight hours, providing accessible locations, and so forth. But programmers must remember that most older individuals have vision and hearing problems. In addition, the lack of a lifelong association with computers and even TV among the elderly may hinder use of these media for educational purposes.

Finally, as with other age groups, the appeal of continuing education for older Americans is strongest among those of a certain social-occupational status. As a result, the older adult who can be described as lower class, blue collar, and/or minority frequently does not participate in educational activities.

7   Programming
for the Disadvantaged

In the two decades following World War II, Americans were sensitized to the condition of a large portion of the population that was later to become identified as the "disadvantaged." Subsequently, the disadvantaged have been defined in a variety of ways, including by physical condition, economic status, and educational level. Some definitions include all individuals who are aged, disabled, poor, members of a minority group, or who have a limited education, but the most frequently applied definitions are based on two criteria: economics and educational achievement level. Early application of these criteria characterized the disadvantaged as individuals who were in the lowest socioeconomic class and who had completed less than eight grades of school.

More recently, the National Advisory Council on Adult Education (NACAE) developed a broader concept of the "larger population" for adult basic education (ABE) primarily based on an educational achievement level. The target population is thus defined as including those 50 million adults 16 years of age or older who have not completed high school (NACAE, 1974). The target population concept was developed by the Research Committee of the NACAE. In 1971 the council began to examine the extensive array of problems associated with delivering services to the educationally disadvantaged. The depth of the problem is vividly illustrated by the fact that ABE programs *enroll* only slightly more individuals each year than the number who drop out of high school without obtaining a diploma (NACAE, 1974).

The target population identified by the NACAE possesses two characteristics: a lower-than-average school achievement level and a higher-than-average number at the lower levels of the American economy and society. Phenomena related to socioeconomic status affect the target population in seven ways:

1. Lower levels of schooling often prevent people from working at all. Less than half of the group was in the labor force, a rate which was fully 25 percent below that of the whole population 16 and over.
2. Lower levels of schooling generate higher rates of dependency. More than 3.3 million of the target group were receiving public assistance.
3. Even when able to participate in the labor force, those with below average schooling showed significantly higher rates of unemployment and higher proportions of part-time work than their counterparts with high school diplomas.
4. The new occupational and industrial environment in America has increased job opportunities in the professional, managerial, clerical, sales, and skilled occupations and in the service-producing sectors of the economy. Demands for more schooling in these fields hamper the entrance of millions of workers with less than 12 years of education.
5. The jobs requiring more schooling pay better. Even among members of the target population who did work, half had annual incomes under $5,000 and half a million had to be on welfare while working.
6. Large numbers of Americans move, mostly in response to economic opportunity. Higher mobility rates are found among those with higher levels of schooling, indicating that millions of people cannot respond to the changing geography of employment opportunity.
7. Technological development in a country depends on the quality of its labor force and particularly on training and education. In turn, technology affects the kinds of jobs which a country provides for its workers. The evidence shows that a trained and educated work force finds better jobs and more job satisfaction. Thus, the people left behind on the educational front have been at a severe disadvantage in the current world of work. The prospects are as bleak for them as well in the 1980s.

Government projections point to a continued expansion of jobs in the white collar, skilled, and service fields, at least through 1990. They also point to the continued need for people to be flexible and adaptable to these changes, to expected technological advances, and to changes in the location of employment opportunity.

Despite impressive recent changes in educational profiles of different segments of the American population such as the rising level of educational attainment among blacks, educational programs for disadvantaged adults are designed to address a critical need. Unfortunately, there are many reasons to believe that the need for such programs will not decrease in the foreseeable future. Although the relative proportion of older adults and blacks without high school diplomas may be reduced, as long as the population continues to increase, and large numbers of youths leave school prior to completion, many adults will need ABE remedial education of some kind.

Several subtopics related to programs for the disadvantaged are developed in this chapter. We will discuss the following: (a) characteristics of the disadvantaged, (b) employment and unemployment, (c) history of programs for the disadvantaged, (d) curricula, and (e) criticism of the programs.

CHARACTERISTICS OF THE DISADVANTAGED

The population defined as disadvantaged has been the subject of numerous investigations. Some conclusions and information reported in selected studies are discussed here to illustrate some of the attributes of the disadvantaged that have implications for adult and continuing education. Knowledge and understanding of the characteristics of the disadvantaged population should inform the process of planning and managing adult and continuing education programs. Wells provides five characteristics of this group.

1. The disadvantaged adults often have become apathetic as a result of numerous failures in previous efforts.
2. The disadvantaged adults are likely to suffer from poor self-concepts.
3. The disadvantaged adults will often show hostility toward institutions which can help them the most because of previous real or imagined experiences in dealing with them.
4. The disadvantaged adults are fearful of authority.

5. The disadvantaged adults trust neither those around them nor those in a position to assist them.   (1972, p. 14)

Disadvantaged adult students may be considered to be biologically deprived. Their social group is marked by a high incidence of birth defects, illness, poor diet, and employment requiring high expenditures of physical energy. Disadvantaged children have been described as coming from homes where the primary need is for the services of a nurse, a dentist, or a dietician and where many kinds of psychological problems beset family members. It has been suggested that it is absurd to try to get such students to focus their attention on ancient history, multiplication tables, or parts of speech when common sense demands a concern with situations under which they live.

The disadvantaged may also be psychologically deprived because living conditions apparently affect mental development. Tuckman (1967) reports a study by Dennis revealing that many children in a Teheran orphanage had not walked by the time they were four years of age. It is believed that in a barren environment, there is less stimulation for developing psychomotor skills as well as for cognitive, perceptual, and verbal skills. Tuckman further suggests that in a culturally deprived home, the immediate gratification of biological needs requires much energy and emotional involvement by parents. Consequently, little energy remains for the development of their children's intelligence.

The disadvantaged usually appear to lack motivation to achieve. The phenomenon of limited motivation is paralleled by the existence of unfavorable attitudes toward self, others, and the world.

EMPLOYMENT AND UNEMPLOYMENT

A persistent correlation exists between education and participation in the labor market. In general, higher levels of school achievement are accompanied by higher rates of labor force involvement. The spread is very large. The rate of labor market participation for those with the most school—five years of college—is almost four times that of the group with the least years completed. There is a difference of more than 20 percentage points between the rates of elementary school and high school graduates. The only exception to this correlation is found among those who go to college but do not graduate. Their labor market participation rates are lower than those of both high school and college graduates. The same phenomenon is also found among some groups who enter high school but do not finish. Their rates are also often lower than those of either the elementary school or high school graduate (NACAE, 1974).

The same pattern holds for both men and women and for whites and nonwhites. Since World War II, women have joined the labor force in rising numbers, particularly in the white collar occupations and service-producing industries. They have added significantly to the worker resources in the country as well as to national and family incomes. Their achievement also has been intimately related to school attainment. For example, among single women, who can be expected to enter the job market in considerable numbers, the lack of schooling can be a strong barrier to employment. Even among married women, where worker rates are generally lower, schooling makes a big difference.

Evidence supports the proposition that school attainment is a major factor affecting worker rates among various age groups. Among men 35 to 44, just about everyone works who can. This age group has the highest participation rate—96 percent. Yet, in this category the rate for men who had less than five years of school was only 84 percent in contrast with 97 percent for the high school graduate and 99 percent for the college graduate (NACAE, 1974).

The impact of schooling on employment becomes an even greater selective barrier among older age groups. There is thus considerable room for program development at the upper end of the age range even though many people in this age group may already be in retirement (NACAE, 1974). Even in a group where people already have attained what is generally considered retirement age, almost half of the men with advanced education are still in the labor force, more than triple the proportion at the other end of the educational spectrum (Northcutt, 1975). Among women of this age, about one of every four with advanced schooling is still in the labor force, quadruple the corresponding ratio for those with less than five years of school. High school graduates among both men and women 65 and over are still active in the work force in significant proportions, well above what prevails for those with no more than an elementary school education.

The condition of literacy in America is further revealed by the adult performance level (APL) study published at the University of Texas. The study, designated to determine how well American adults from all walks of life with a range of educational achievement, could function in modern society, produced some disquieting results. About 20 percent of the adult population were found to be functionally incompetent. Many people could not perform simple tasks such as reading a want ad, addressing an envelope, or calculating the change due on a purchase. Thirty-nine million people, another 34 percent of the adult population, were found to be barely functional in these basic activities (Copperman, 1978).

PROGRAM HISTORY

The concept of providing literacy education for adults has a long and fertile history. Programs designed to reach illiterate adults and youth have been financed by governmental and charitable organizations and offered by proprietary institutions. In the American colonies, the ability to read was important because it enabled people to study the Bible. It was also evident that in the developing nation economic benefits could be associated with literacy skills. Early in the social life of the English colonies in America, the church and private schools were important institutions in the education of adults and youth (Long, 1976).

Private evening schools designed to teach reading, writing, computation, and other subjects were popular in eighteenth-century coastal cities, and many apprentices studied in them. Because of the scarcity of young men available as apprentices in colonial America, they could negotiate better contracts than could their English cousins. As a consequence most apprenticeship contracts of the eighteenth century included a "schooling" clause. Masters were required to teach apprentices how to read and write, and they preferred to send them to the evening schools for this purpose. Following this procedure masters had the service of apprentices during working hours, and apprentices had their freedom in the evening. It seems to have been a good arrangement for all concerned (Long, 1976). Nevertheless, schooling was often limited in frontier communities.

Beginning in the late nineteenth century, we note the first governmental efforts to address literacy education. Evening schools were established in some large cities for adult learners. Limited federal funds for literacy programs were made available in 1918 with the passage of the Immigration and Nationality Act. That legislation provided monies to assist public schools in the teaching of English, history, government, and citizenship to candidates for naturalization.

After the national census of 1920, an increased awareness of the literacy problem developed. The census data revealed that large numbers of immigrants in the urban centers of the North and poor rural native Americans of the South were illiterate. From about 1910 to 1930, a number of philanthropic efforts were initiated to reduce the rural literacy problem in the Southern states. Among these were Martha Berry College in Rome, Georgia, and the South Carolina Opportunity School in Columbia. In addition "moonlight" and "lay-by" schools also were conducted in many Southern states while evening schools were provided in the urban North. The moonlight schools received their name from the fact that they were open at night. The lay-by schools were day schools conducted for a few weeks in early summer between the last cultivation of agricultural crops and the beginning of harvest.

Even though many state departments of education adopted literacy campaigns in the 1920s and 1930s, efforts to provide educational opportunities for disadvantaged adults were frequently sporadic and poorly financed. By the 1960s, however, adult basic education had developed into a reputable part of many public school programs. Cortwright and Brice (1970) report that more than 80 percent of public school teachers surveyed responded that the schools should provide adult education programs. The Economic Opportunity Act of 1964 is identified as the legislation that provided the necessary federal support desired by adult and continuing educators. Two years later, the Adult Education Act of 1966, adopted as Title II of the Elementary and Secondary Education Act amendments, provided even firmer legitimization of governmental support for literacy education. Adult basic education legislation was also incorporated in Title VI of the education amendments of 1974. The 1974 law extended the provisions of earlier legislation, providing for bilingual adult education programs, programs for institutionalized adults, and the establishment of state advisory committees on adult education. The 1974 legislation also gave the state departments of education direct control over funds used for experimental demonstration projects and staff development activities.

The 1978 amendments to the Adult Education Act mandate the

states to carry out vigorous programs of outreach for those most in need of basic instruction, to provide assistance to potential students such as flexible schedules, transportation, and child care help, and to consult with a broad range of interests and organizations in the presentation of state plans and in their implementation (NACAE, 1980).

CURRICULA

Four major models illustrate the dimensions and character of programs for the disadvantaged as addressed by educational institutions. The models may be defined as (a) traditional, (b) APL, (c) functional, and (d) English as a second language. Each is briefly discussed in the following pages. Exhaustive treatment of each concept is not consistent with the overall objectives of this volume: The reader who has a deep interest in the topic will find adequate discussion of each model elsewhere.

TRADITIONAL

Federal legislation authorizing funds for literacy education implies that the illiterate person needs two kinds of knowledge to cope with the present and short-term future occupational situation. These are literacy skills and a basic core of concepts, facts, and attitudes related to upward mobility. The latter includes (a) an introduction to the world of work, (b) good health and hygiene practices, (c) consumer education, (d) basic citizenship concepts, and (e) awareness of personal-social development skills. When these concepts and related knowledge are properly implemented, the basic education programs are designed to meet as nearly as possible the student's needs, including attitude change, whose fulfillment is vital to the work and educational success of so many basic education students. In the stronger programs, the basic education curriculum is designed to meet the adult learner's needs, and most of the instruction is individualized.

The ABE content curriculum often includes the five core areas just listed. Within these broad topics, ABE instruction focuses on such things as attitudes toward work, accident prevention, money management, job interviewing, voting rights, welfare and Social Security services, and hobby development. At the same time, students should also be developing their basic training skills and their social skills (Smith & Martin, 1972).

After the broad outline of a curriculum has been determined, specific topics need to be selected and ways for developing them determined. Some sample topics within several areas have been given for illustrative purposes. Of course all topics will not be used with all students, but the larger the array from which to choose, the more likelihood there is of meeting student needs.

Mezirow et al. (1975) have described the content of ABE classes based on extensive surveys and observations made in 1971. They report that instruction in such areas as health, family life, and consumer and civic education is only incidental to other teaching, although the official goals of ABE encourage instruction in these areas. There is some disagreement on the emphasis given to "coping skills"; Mezirow et al. found instruction in these areas only on rare occasions. They note, however, that state directors of ABE programs contradict their observations.

Orem (1973) reports an interesting study designed to determine the correlation between the social class of teachers and emphasis on nontraditional versus traditional curricular topics. He defined arithmetic and communication skills as traditional content; nontraditional content was defined as health education, consumer education, ethnic heritage, and coping skills. Orem concluded that teachers from lower economic backgrounds tend to place a greater emphasis on health and consumer education topics than do teachers from higher socioeconomic levels. Black teachers placed a greater emphasis on all four nontraditional topics than did white teachers; the strongest association was with ethnic heritage and the weakest was with coping skills.

ESL classes were identified (Mezirow et al., 1975) as the ones generally placing greater emphasis on socialization skills. The authors assert that the tradition of Americanization instruction provides precedent for the approach. Therefore, ESL teachers are regularly concerned with American customs, problems, and values through discussion of topics such as consumerism, race relations, birth control, and U.S. foreign policy.

APL

A different curriculum approach is reflected in the adult performance level concept. Based on work conducted at the University of Texas, five skill areas and five content areas are identified for basic education programs. The skill areas are identification of facts and terms, reading, writing, comparisons, and problem solving. The content areas, which address each of the skill areas, are identified as community resources, occupational knowledge, consumer economics, health and government, and law. For example, a needed reading skill associated with occupational knowledge is the ability to read a want ad. Computational skills may include the ability to figure one's expected earnings based on an hourly wage rate. Computation and consumer economics are identified in the APL data as the areas in which the greatest number of adults function with difficulty.

FUNCTIONAL

The idea of functional literacy espoused by UNESCO seems to be faintly related to the APL concept. According to UNESCO publications, adult educators do not always communicate clearly about functional literacy; therefore, the topic is subject to distortions (UNESCO, 1970). Unfortunately, the organization's literature also fails to clearly and precisely define functional literacy. It is reported by UNESCO that functional literacy work means any literacy operation conceived as a component of economic and social development projects. The main characteristic that seems to distinguish functional from traditional literacy, states UNESCO, is that it is "no longer . . . isolated or distinct" from other social and economic endeavors (UNESCO, 1970). Other efforts have been made to clarify the concept, but they do not add significantly to our understanding.

ENGLISH AS A SECOND LANGUAGE

The teaching of English as a second language (ESL) is a program area closely related to ABE. Increasing awareness of the immigrant population, legal or otherwise, has contributed to additional support for ESL instruction. ESL is in some ways similar to ABE and in some ways different. The unique dimension of ESL resides in the area of language and the challenge represented by that aspect of the teaching-learning transaction.

Mattran (1979) is of the opinion that four areas in ABE/ESL require immediate and special attention. They are: (a) language assessment, (b) professionalization, (c) classroom materials, and (d) research. Mattran calls for special attention to the problems of aliens who are illiterate in their native tongue. A difficult challenge faces program planners and teachers who seek to meet the needs of this kind of learner. It is likely the immigrants who are not literate — in their native language may also suffer from some of the same kind of negative effects of social marginality experienced by the native American poor.

Mattran (1979) notes that good learning material is limited. That which is available is described as being too linguistically complex for the background of ESL instructors. There is also a need for soundly organized materials so as to provide relevant lessons in English.

Mattran's comment may explain the observation of Mezirow et al. (1975) that ESL teachers often supplemented the limited commercially prepared materials with references to television programs, museum exhibits, magazine articles, and other similar sources of information. Even though there is an emphasis on socialization, ESL teachers tend to follow the elementary school emphasis on teaching reading rather than spoken English. Therefore, the rules of grammar constitute a highly visible element for ESL instruction (Mezirow et al., 1975).

CRITICISM

The disparity between the results of literacy programs for the disadvantaged and educational goals has been a concern around the world. UNESCO (1970) observes that the gap is so great that the most vigorous measures are required to either adjust the latter or improve the former. According to UNESCO the main weakness lies in the lack of sufficient experimentation. Experimentation in the area of literacy/ABE programming is the victim of social forces. First, although the acceptability, if not desirability, of providing "second chance" educational opportunity has increased dramatically, there remain influential politicians and school administrators who relegate ABE to such a low priority that programs are constantly threatened by every budget emergency.

Second, the people served by ABE also contribute indirectly to the program's difficulty. They are frequently powerless, and they

lack political leadership. They often are identified as solely responsible for their condition, and if the condition is to be changed, they
must do it at their own expense. Finally, they demonstrate only
limited interest in programs as they are currently designed.

Large-scale ABE programs require considerable money. The
availability of such financial support is greatly influenced by the kinds
of factors already mentioned. In times when funds are available, ABE
is low in priority and thus obtains limited support. In hard times program budgets are drastically cut. Criticisms of the limited success of
the service and public preferences for other services complicate the
programming process.

Despite the great hopes that gave impetus to ABE, its accom-
plishments have not been consistent with its goals. With more than
24 million functionally illiterate adults almost 20 years after the passage of the Economic Opportunity Act of 1964, the challenge remains
a very real one. The barriers encountered by ABE administrators and
planners include the extremely difficult problems of recruiting the
illiterate adult to enroll in educational activities, disagreements about
the curriculum and ultimate purpose of ABE, and the marginal status
of programs and personnel.

Clark (1980) has charged that ABE programs are not sufficiently responsive to the needs of the disadvantaged. He recommends
six procedures that address the problem: (a) the program design
should be changed to lead more directly to employment, (b) employers should change policies that require more education than is
needed, (c) program content and entrance requirements should be
modified, (d) better counseling is needed, (e) learners must be prepared to confront the system, and (f) programs must be based on
personal characteristics of the learners.

Mezirow et al. (1975) write that dissatisfaction with elements of
ABE programs has led to suggestions for improvement. Some want
to politicize the program, some would vocationalize it, and some
would socialize it by integrating it into a comprehensive program of
social services. Yet others would enhance its academic character:
Based on their national study, Mezirow et al. (1975) suggest a number of specific action imperatives to improve educational processes in
ABE programs. Some of these recommendations are reflected in the
1978 amendments to the Adult Education Act.

SUMMARY AND CONCLUSIONS

This chapter discusses several topics in the area of educational programming for disadvantaged adults. We noted that the concept of "disadvantaged" as used here gradually shifted from socioeconomic criteria to educational ones. Furthermore, the target population for ABE was redefined from adults who had not finished the eighth grade to those who had not finished high school. We also observed that according to the APL study, possession of a high school diploma does not assure competence in basic skills such as reading, writing, and computation.

Limited academic skills and low educational attainment are associated with a variety of negative socioeconomic indexes. Some of the characteristics attributed to the educationally disadvantaged were noted in this chapter.

Illiteracy has long been a problem in American society. The frontier character of the nation for the first 100 years of its history made schooling precious and limited. The second century saw large-scale immigration in the North and economic and social dislocation in the South following the Civil War. Thus, literacy for adults became an important concern both in the Northern industrial cities with their expanding immigrant population and in the capital-poor rural South.

A brief history of educational programs for illiterate American adults reveals the development of state literacy campaigns in the 1920s and 1930s that were later strengthened by federal involvement beginning in the 1960s. The Economic Opportunity Act of 1964 provided a vehicle for the distribution of federal funds supporting adult basic education. Since then additional legislation has provided funds to assist the states with ABE and ESL programs.

A variety of approaches are used in ABE and ESL programs, and each approach has its supporters and detractors. Analyses of these approaches have focused on student-teacher relationships, the curriculum, and the instructional mode.

The disadvantaged population may prove to be the greatest challenge for adult and continuing education. Practitioners must seek new ways of applying the technology of the field and of the new electronic media to this population.

IMPLICATIONS

The concept of *disadvantaged* is a dynamic one. It is likely to continue to change as American society changes. Obviously, modifications of the definition used to determine who is disadvantaged will have an impact on educational programming activities. The potential population will vary directly with the breadth of the concept. Simultaneously, the content, instructional processes, and other program elements such as resources and objectives will be influenced.

Despite the rising educational level of large numbers of Americans, the educational needs of the disadvantaged persist. Economic and political aspects of the problem will have implications for educational activities designed to improve the conditions of the disadvantaged. Unfortunately, current legislation fails to provide the kinds of resources needed to enable the many levels of education to address the different dimensions of the problem. Educators are often left with feelings of helplessness or frustration. Somehow, either government must redefine its role in providing for the education of the disadvantaged or new philanthropic and programming thrusts must be discovered.

8 Programming for Women

From Madison Avenue–inspired advertisements to legal codes adopted in statehouses and the halls of Congress, changes in American society that concern women were visible and numerous in the 1960s. Some significant developments with implications for programming for women in adult and continuing education include the following:

- Women now have the equivalent of a second life. There were formerly two stages in a woman's life: the premarital stage and the period devoted to childbearing and the rearing of children. Today, most women can look forward to a third and longer life phase—the period between ages 35 and 76—as the majority give birth to the last of their children around the age of 30 (Royal Commission on the Status of Women in Canada, 1970).
- Women's employment patterns are changing. For example, 69 percent of women less than 25 years of age were employed in 1980, and women now outnumber men in key service industries such as finance, insurance, real estate, and teaching (Jones, 1980).
- Baby boom mothers have redefined the nature of a woman's lifetime work experience by working during the young years of their children (Jones, 1980). At the same time, the focus for women in continuing education has shifted to future employment (Luther, Hendel, & Mucke, 1981).
- Women are marrying later, and more are remaining single (Jones, 1980). As a result, women 25 to 35 years of age demand more autonomy and a greater sense of self than was characteristic of their mothers (Luther, Hendel, & Mucke, 1981).
- The seventies were an exciting period. During the decade America's postwar babies, born during those halcyon years of 1946–1957, achieved adulthood. It is the generation that has been branded with labels such as war babies, Pepsi generation, me generation, and

flower children. It has been described as the largest, the richest, and the best-educated generation in American history. It was the first generation to experience jet airplanes, television, and space flight, and it is also the generation that participated in a series of efforts described as the "democratization" of America. Its members developed values of human dignity and worth and greatly prized equality and equity.

The women's movement emerged in full force through the strength of numbers found in the baby boom generation. These women did not create the social movement toward recognition of changing roles and relationships, but they gave it a "mass" heretofore absent. They also contributed to other changes in society that coupled economic and political pragmatism with modified social values. The combination of changing social, political, and economic roles of women since 1942 in many Western nations has directly affected adult and continuing education programs.

Sexual discrimination, women's liberation, and the changing roles and life-styles of women received unparalleled attention in the 1970s. Changes in social customs, politics, economic behavior, and interpersonal relations encompassed a variety of activities that spilled over into continuing education for women. "Awareness" became a key concept in what became identified as the women's movement—consciousness raising was its synonym. Whatever the cause, there is little question that during the same period mature women became involved in educational activities at unprecedented levels.

The phenomenon identified as continuing education for women (CEW) is interesting as a reflection of the growth and emergence of a sociopolitical force in American politics associated with the civil rights movement, concern for the elderly, vocational rehabilitation, rights of the handicapped, criminal rehabilitation, and an awareness of the injustices perpetrated on the American Indian. It is also an interesting and fascinating topic on its own merits. The following pages discuss topics concerning the availability, development, and future of continuing education for women. We shall briefly examine: (a) the history of CEW, (b) some reasons behind the return to college, (c) the rising desire to work among adult women, (d) educational services for women, (e) an overview of women's programs, (f) a description of the female adult learner, (g) contemporary CEW developments, and (h) counseling in CEW.

HISTORY

Two centuries ago, Abigail Adams made eloquent comments on the subject of equal education for women. Jefferson and Franklin took pains to encourage their daughters' education even before the establishment of women's seminaries and boarding schools (Long, 1975). Nevertheless, the emergence of continuing education for women as a distinctive program area is rightly viewed as a twentieth-century phenomenon.

The growth of women's participation in adult and continuing education from 1961 to 1978 is documented. For example, Johnstone and Rivera (1965), reporting the National Opinion Research Clinic (NORC) survey conducted in 1961–1962, conclude that the adult participant in education was as likely to be a woman as a man. More recent data reported by the National Center for Education Statistics (1980) show that more women than men are engaged in continuing education. While women's programs do not account for all the increase in women's participation, it is obvious that the specific program area experienced rapid growth in the past 10 years. The Women's Bureau of the U.S. Department of Labor reported that the number of programs especially for women increased from 250 in 1968 to approximately 450 in 1971 and to over 500 in 1974 (U.S. Department of Labor, 1971, 1974).

The trend toward greater educational participation of women is also revealed through statistics concerning college enrollments.

THE RETURN TO COLLEGE

The number of women and girls seeking a college education has dramatically increased. In the fall of 1969, women college students numbered 3,222,000 (U.S. Department of Health, Education and Welfare, 1969)—more than four times greater than in 1950. During this period the population of girls aged 18 to 21 increased less than 60 percent. The marked gain in school attendance extended to adult women as well as college-age girls. Between 1950 and 1972, school enrollment rose from 26,000 to 281,000 among women aged 25 to 29 and from 21,000 to 200,000 among women 30 to 34 (U.S. Department of Labor, 1974).

The interest of mature women in postsecondary education is believed to be related to a greater desire of Americans in every age group to develop their understanding of the complexities of modern life. There is a widespread realization that additional education can bring deeper personal enrichment as well as job skills useful in the working world (U.S. Department of Commerce, 1970).

Various demographic factors also help to explain the interest of mature American women in college attendance and the even greater interest among women than among men over 35 years of age. These factors include women's early age at marriage, the frequent changes in their pattern of living, and their lengthened life-span.

Large numbers of women leave college before graduation in order to help finance the education of their husbands or to care for their homes and children. Although studies that trace college freshmen from initial enrollment through graduation are not available, data reported by the Women's Bureau of the U.S. Department of Labor (1971) indicate nearly 50 percent of women may drop out of college without completing a baccalaureate degree in a four-year period.

True dropout rates cannot be calculated because many freshmen are part-time students, some are enrolled in five-year programs, and others terminate their schooling after graduating from a two-year college. Nevertheless, it is significant that the number who graduate is much smaller than the number who enrolled in college four years earlier. Thus, it is evident that many of the women who did not graduate are potential "returnees" during their mature years.

When home and family responsibilities lessen, many women find they have time to resume formal education. Some women are interested in returning to school for cultural or social reasons while others wish to attain a higher degree, to update their professional skills, or to prepare for reentering the work force. Refresher courses, as well as courses that are completely new, can update job skills made obsolete by technological, scientific, or other advances.

RISING JOB INTEREST OF ADULT WOMEN

U.S. labor statistics also document a tremendous increase in the number of mature women who are working outside the home. The stimulus is often a desire to supplement family income. Women's salaries help send children to college, buy homes, pay medical bills, or meet routine expenses. Those who are divorced or widowed often must work to support themselves and dependents. The need for the services of educated and talented persons in a variety of challenging occupations is also attracting women into the work force who heretofore may have preferred to use their time in other ways.

In 1969 there were 30.5 million women workers 16 years of age and over, as contrasted with 18.4 million in 1950. Less than half of the 12-million increase is attributed to the larger number of women in the population; the remainder is attributed to the greater tendency of women to enter the work force (U.S. Department of Commerce, 1970).

EDUCATIONAL SERVICES

Reports of the educational interests and problems of adult women, though somewhat dated, are available in two questionnaire surveys conducted by the Women's Bureau of the Department of Labor. Both were follow-up studies of women who had been out of college for some years.

The more recent of these surveys was conducted in 1964 among women who graduated from college in June 1957 (U.S. Department of Labor, 1966). The interest in continuing education and in paid employment was exceedingly high both among the 51 percent in the work force in 1964 and among the 49 percent out of it. Of the total group, almost three-fourths said they were planning to enroll in an educational or training course in the future. Of these, more than half were motivated by job-connected reasons; the others had cultural or personal interests. Although 46 percent of the June 1957 women graduates had taken at least one graduate or professional course in the seven years since graduation, few commented on the adequacy of their educational opportunities or suggested improvements.

More revealing clues to the educational experiences of adult women were provided in the Women's Bureau exploratory survey among women who had been out of college for 15 years (U.S. Department of Labor, 1962). As most of this group had children in school, many were at an age when they were thinking of changing their pattern of living. When surveyed, about one-third of the women were employed and five-sixths of the remainder indicated interest in future employment. Many also expressed a desire for additional education and training; university courses that would prepare them for teaching were particularly desirable at that time.

Women with recent experience in university courses were critical of those with methodology and content directed at teenagers. Such courses do not satisfy women with considerable life experience. Other women reported having difficulty in locating classes that reviewed and updated basic information in their fields of interest.

Classes offered by local colleges were not convenient for some mothers who wanted courses scheduled when they were not caring for their children. They preferred to attend classes during the daytime school hours, in the evening, on Saturday, or in the summertime. Some alumnae also expressed an interest in accelerated courses when they were preparing for employment. Time schedules arranged principally for young people sometimes made them impatient.

The most frequent request of the survey respondents was for individual counseling by qualified persons. College counselors who necessarily spend most of their time working with teenagers were perceived as not being sensitive to the special problems associated with continuing family responsibilities and reentry into the labor force at a mature age. The women also felt that many counselors were not aware of existing services and facilities that could help them.

The various suggestions and criticisms made by these college alumnae shed light on the special interests of mature women who are continuing their education. The responses also raised doubts about the adequacy of many courses and services available to mature women in colleges and universities (U.S. Department of Labor, 1971).

AN OVERVIEW OF WOMEN'S PROGRAMS

Holt (1980) has addressed three major questions asked by personnel in adult and continuing education: (a) What are women's programs? (b) Why do we need them? and (c) What factors should we consider for maximum participation in women's programs?

WHAT ARE WOMEN'S PROGRAMS?

Holt defines women's programs as activities that are specifically designed for women and promoted for their participation. Accordingly, these programs are related to issues, experiences, and concerns that are generally perceived to be unique to women; issues that traditionally have been examined from a male perspective; or programs that have arisen out of contemporary social change. Examples include programs that deal with biological and psychological subjects such as menopause and mother-daughter relationships and topics like sexual harassment (Holt, 1980). Holt observes that topics that traditionally have been viewed from a male perspective, and which have only recently become attractive to women, include estate planning, automotive mechanics, and building investments. Women and math anxiety, women in management, and women in politics are cited as types of programs that she believes illustrate special interests arising out of contemporary social change that are influencing women's roles in society.

Holt does not believe women's programs are or should be designed to separate the sexes. "But," she says, "they are developed for a single-sex clientele because they biologically are of most direct concern to females, deal with issues historically eliminated from women's learning experiences, or concern areas where women were commonly denied admittance or at least not encouraged to pursue" (1980, p. 1).

The Need for Women's Programs

The need for continuing education activities for women has been expressed in a variety of ways. They may be justified as a means to address career transitions and to provide information concerned with new research into biological and psychological development. Other programs may also be required to examine, from a woman's point of view, areas that are believed to have been treated historically from a male perspective (Holt, 1980). The need for separate programs on topics such as legal status and financial matters may decline, according to Holt (1980). However, she believes that social changes that will obviate the need will be slow in arriving.

Factors to Consider for Maximum Participation

Planners of educational programs for women may wish to consider three questions:

1. What social-economic variables are relevant to the programs being planned for women?
2. What economic and labor trends are related to women's issues?
3. What kind of programs are suggested by research surveys and polls concerning attitudes, values, and needs? (Holt, 1980, p. 3)

ILLUSTRATIVE CEW PROGRAMS

Courses instituted following World War II were forerunners of continuing education programs for women. College graduates with a background in liberal arts were given intensive courses in education leading to teacher certification. Some colleges and universities also scheduled refresher courses for professional nurses (U.S. Department of Labor, 1971).

The continuing education programs developed for women in the 1960s acquired interesting new features including limited course loads in degree or nondegree programs, flexible scheduling of classes at hours convenient for housewives, and liberal provision for transfer credits, educational and employment counseling, financial assistance for part-time study, nursery services, and job placement services.

In 1960 the University of Minnesota formally organized a facility specifically committed to making the resources of the university more useful to adult women. Now called the Minnesota Planning and Counseling Center for Women, it highlights individual counseling and information services for women at all levels of education. Women are referred to both educational and employment opportunities throughout the local metropolitan area. This comprehensive program also encompasses scholarship aid for adult women, nursery facilities, and job placement services.

Interest in assisting mature women was also revealed in activities of various service-oriented organizations. For example, in 1950 the Hannah Harrison School was opened in Washington, D.C., under the auspices of the local Young Women's Christian Association. Free tuition, room, and board are provided the women selected to participate in one of the several job-training programs run by the school.

In 1952 the Altrusa International Foundation set up a vocational aid project to provide financial assistance to older women having difficulties in obtaining employment. In Minneapolis, the Career Clinic for Mature Women was established in 1958 to provide pre-employment counseling and training programs for older women. Since then various women's organizations, community associations, high schools, state and local government agencies, and private groups have developed special services or programs for mature women.

A program especially advantageous for adult women would facilitate their resumption of an interrupted college education. Sarah Lawrence College in New York initiated such a program in 1962, accenting the resumption of undergraduate study on a part-time basis. The women are provided counseling assistance and refresher courses prior to admission as degree candidates. The enthusiastic response to the program stimulated the establishment of part-time arrangements for graduate study as well.

General orientation workshops and courses have been developed in response to widespread demand from adult women interested in entering or reentering the work force. These courses typically provide guest lectures on careers, information about courses and volunteer work, counseling on both a group and an individual basis, and placement assistance. Noteworthy because of their relatively low fees are the fairly new orientation courses offered by the public school systems in several localities.

The Radcliffe Institute in Massachusetts seeks highly qualified women, particularly those with advanced degrees, and provides generous financial assistance so they can combine a period of creative study with homemaking. Its expanded program also includes two other fellowship programs, weekly seminars for adult women, a guidance laboratory, and a research program.

Many colleges and universities, of course, arrange programs and services that benefit both adult men and adult women. In addition, private business, trade, and technical schools provide training programs advantageously scheduled from the viewpoint of adult women. Since these schools generally specialize in training for employment, they usually offer short-term, intensive, and practical courses. Often classes are held both day and night and can be taken on a full- or part-time basis. Tuition varies widely, ranging from very modest to relatively high fees.

THE FEMALE ADULT LEARNER

The University of Minnesota (n.d.) has described participants in its continuing education program for women. Data generated by 1,134 respondents who had enrolled for at least one course or one service provided by the program were interpreted as follows:

- The average age at initial contact was about 39. Participants were likely to be white. They had diverse economic backgrounds, but their median household income was about $35,000. They perceived their health to be good.
- More than 50 percent of the respondents held a baccalaureate degree.
- Slightly over 60 percent of the respondents were employed.
- A majority of the respondents indicate they believe their talents are not used very well.
- Most of the respondents were reported as being happy with life, but women who were unemployed and looking for work, as well as women who were working at a job that did not require a college degree, were reported to be significantly less satisfied (University of Minnesota, n.d., p. 2).

CONTEMPORARY DEVELOPMENTS

Just as CEW programs emerged from social change, their modification and continuation are influenced by social, psychological, and technological developments. For example, after rapid approval by a number of states, the proposed Equal Rights Amendment encountered stubborn social resistance. Changing economic conditions also contributed to a reduction in federal money available to subsidize women's programs. In light of these and other developments, what is the current condition of women's programs?

In the spring of 1981, I mailed a short survey form to 50 institutions reporting women's continuing education programs. Approximately 20 program directors and other administrators responded to the survey. The respondents were evenly divided: Half said that women's programs at their institutions were increasing in number, and half found such programs to be decreasing. Several respondents attributed the decrease to competition from outside programs offered by all kinds of organizations. One respondent said, "My personal feeling is that there are now so many groups offering women's programs that they have tended to dissipate and hurt each other. Had just colleges, or universities, or community colleges offered programs, it might have been better. However, YWCAs, NOW organizations, Women's Clubs, PTAs and everybody got into the business, and thus the women who did want to take a program or a course are so fragmented that groups are not obtaining successful enrollments." Another respondent said, "Women's programs have decreased in popularity because of the overavailability." A third program leader said, "So many agencies and organizations are programming for women now, in contrast to our early years, that we in University Extension sometimes see lower enrollments in our own programs. It is obvious that vastly more women are interested in 'women's issues' than ever before." The majority of those who addressed the question, however, indicated that women's programs continue to be well attended. Two responses were obtained from organizations in the same city. One respondent indicated that women's programs were increasing while the other indicated that her organization was experiencing some difficulty.

The above data suggest that the success of CEW programs is uneven. The responses confirm the popularity of programming for women, but they also suggest that the market may be becoming saturated. The implications of market saturation are even more significant when financial problems are considered. For example, more than half of the respondents reported that financing women's programs is difficult. Most respondents implied that few of the programs were financially successful. The programs were often cited as requiring subsidies from the university budget or grants from foundations or the government.

In an effort to improve the profit picture by addressing needs perceived to be more pertinent to women of the 1980s, about half of the respondents indicate their program offerings have changed. Most of those reporting changes note that their early programming featured personal fulfillment, leisure activities, consciousness raising, and intellectual enrichment. The focus has shifted to what one respondent called "more pragmatic topics" such as employment and finances.

Characteristics of the participants in women's programs were reported to be quite varied. They seem to be in general agreement with the findings of the University of Minnesota study described earlier.

Societal attitudes, which are reflected in local support for CEW programs, also varied among the respondents. At best, it seems that the attitudes are mixed; few respondents found full support. There were several observations about "conservative" opposition or the possibility of "backlash." One respondent said attitudes are "changing" but did not indicate the direction of the change.

One other trend worthy of attention concerns a move toward continuing education programs for "people" as opposed to "women" or "men." A number of respondents indicated that some mixed-sex programs were successful while others suggested that future programs should focus on the "person" rather than a specific sex. Approximately one-third of the respondents volunteered comments of this nature. Other potential program changes, according to the respondents, concern women's roles as single parents and heads of households, role conflict, and the handling of stress. The national economy and the mixed societal attitudes, however, were cited by approximately one-third of the respondents as a threat to future programming in continuing education for women.

The respondents were unanimous in their praise for the "success" of women's programs. One respondent noted, "Our programs have succeeded to the extent that they have encouraged women to look at their lives and their roles to see if they fit the individual life plan for the women." Another observed that "programs have helped women to develop more positive self-image, role clarification, [and] increase skills." Another said, however, "One-day conferences give publicity and raise awareness of women's issues, but they do not go very far to help women gain new skills." Other respondents also commented on the "visibility" conferences give to women's issues. Another individual said, "I believe that the programs have helped women to get a firmer footing in society and to evaluate their own circumstances more realistically. They have given women new confidence and the self-assurance to move ahead and to consider themselves on equal footing with men. Perhaps [we should] encourage women to enroll in all programs . . . rather than singling out programs specifically for women."

COUNSELING: A NEEDED SERVICE

The future of women's programming seems to be related to counseling programs. As noted earlier, women returning to school require advice in the areas of course work, careers, and family life. Continuing educational programs for women are incomplete without an adequate counseling dimension.

The need for counseling appears explicitly or implicitly in much of the literature concerned with women's continuing education. Some of the reasons are as follows:

- Many women have been away from the formal learning experience for years.
- The educational careers of many women have consisted of a patchwork of experiences in several locations.
- Many women learners experience some role conflict.
- Many women returning to the educational arena require assurance and support.
- Many women who wish to renew their educational programs are unsure of their goals and abilities.

Another writer may very well identify a different set of justifications for counseling services for women. The important concern at this point, however, is the recognition of the desirability of such service.

SUMMARY AND CONCLUSIONS

This chapter presents a discussion of topics associated with educational programming for women. It provides an overview of women's programs in which we also attempt to answer the question, What are women's programs? The need for educational activities for women is examined, and some factors concerning maximum participation are discussed. Finally, some illustrative continuing education programs for women are noted.

The emergence and modifications of women's educational programs in the United States provide an excellent example of how social change contributes to programming in adult and continuing education. Early educational programs for women primarily provided liberal arts experiences to college graduates. With the broad social changes that accompanied the civil rights activism and shifting economic conditions of the 1960s, educational programs for women emerged on a broader scale. Some of the first programs were concerned specifically with subjects associated with women's attitudes, such as self-awareness and consciousness raising. More recently, the programs have addressed problems and issues associated with economics and career concerns. There is also limited evidence that the target population has been broadened to include wider socioeconomic representation among participants.

IMPLICATIONS

The future directions of educational programs for women are unclear. One scenario retains the emphasis on women's issues as described by Holt (1980). Another broadens the programming to "person" and family-oriented topics. There is a possibility that the major emphasis will be placed on counseling assistance with content being either women- or "person"-centered. Increasing competition from numerous agencies and organizations may cause universities to design programs that serve as models to be initiated by the other agencies. Changing social attitudes may also contribute to reduced visibility and support for women's programs.

PART IV

New Program Elements and Speculations

Overview

Educational programs over the past 200 years were either successful or unsuccessful in interacting with larger movements on the social, economic, and political stage. The more successful programs were flexible and responsive; administrators and staff were sensitive to changing aspirations, characteristics, and values in American society. Pragmatically, institutional missions were modified, delivery systems altered, and new content provided in different modalities.

No period of American history, however, has reflected changes as deep and as pervasive as the period in which we now chart our course. The word *revolutionary* continues to repeat itself in the language of futurists, scientists, authors, and politicians. Part IV contains two short chapters that discuss some of the implications of contemporary developments on program provision in adult and continuing education.

Nontraditional approaches to education came upon the American scene in 1970–1973 with the force of a tidal wave. Significant changes in attitudes and structures emerged. No longer was "education" limited to "school-

ing"; experience, on-the-job training, and character were
recognized in efforts to "certify" knowledge. Chapter 9
discusses some of the events of the 1970s now labeled as
nontraditional education.

The last chapter of the section, and the final chapter
in the book, contains speculations about future events
in adult and continuing education. Issues and challenges
that face the field are noted. It is once again observed
that all the signposts do not conveniently point in the
same direction. In some instances, interpreting the present
and predicting the future is like experiencing conflicting
traffic directions at a five-cornered intersection. Different
scenarios will be developed by educational programmers
at different institutions, but the more successful programs
will be those that are informed both by the history of
adult and continuing education and by a sensitivity to the
present and future.

9 The Certification of Learning

This seems to be an ideal place to remind ourselves that programming in adult and continuing education includes elements such as learning goals, content, place, time, and, often, evaluation and certification of learning. Just as it is frequently very difficult to disentangle psychological and social developments, it is also often difficult to separate educational practices from the larger society. Consequently, we should not be surprised to observe that a number of developments concerning the certification of learning have become conspicuous in recent years; years already characterized as a time of change.

Developments concerning the certification of learning that have implications for programming in adult and continuing education include the following:

- Increasing demand for and acceptance of awarding educational credits for experience
- Improving technology for reviewing, analyzing, and granting of credit for work and other related experiences
- Increasing emphasis upon some form of "certified" learning experience
- Acceptance of CEU and other similar procedures for recognizing noncredit educational activities
- Impact of military-related training activities
- Difficulties in completing educational programs at one institution caused by mobility

A number of years ago, Houle (1961) provided a typology of orientations of adult learners. He placed orientations in three classes: activity, goal, and learning as briefly described in chapter 3. It is obvious that many people participate in educational activities because they have certain goals that seem to be best attained through education. The learner frequently wants to obtain answers to some specific question, to develop or strengthen a particular skill, or to obtain some kind of certification of competence. This chapter is concerned with the third motivation and the way society, particularly education, has responded.

Following World War II, American higher education became more democratic in terms of accessibility. Veterans entered classrooms in record numbers, and community colleges grew at the rate of one a week for several years. Nevertheless, higher education continued to be beyond the reach of some. Often geographic mobility interfered with continuous enrollment, work schedules prevented adults from attending college, or other personal and family obligations temporarily displaced education as a high-priority activity. At the same time, the growing proportion of Americans holding college degrees was associated with increasing basic entry qualifications for many occupations while advancement in others became tied to educational certificates.

The teaching profession is one of the most visible illustrations of the phenomenon. Prior to World War II, many schoolteachers did not possess a baccalaureate degree, but by the mid-1950s, several states required a master's degree for entry certification. Currently, advancement and even maintenance of teaching credentials are directly related to some kind of "certified" learning activity provided by a higher education institution or some other approved agency.

In the lifetime of the current generation, Americans have developed a three-part "system" of education. The first and oldest part is composed of traditionally oriented schools and colleges. The second part is made up of the nontraditionally oriented schools and colleges that evolved from the former. Finally, the third part consists of "related" institutions such as business and other agencies.

Before we discuss the evolving nontraditional approaches to higher education, a brief comment concerning the "related" system is appropriate. First, this segment of education is believed to be larger than commonly recognized. Large corporations such as American

Telephone and Telegraph (AT&T), International Business Machines (IBM), and General Motors maintain very large and extensive educational programs.

The size of the educational programs maintained by the large corporations is made understandable through comparison. AT&T annually spends more than $1 billion on its education and training program; this is four times the amount spent in comparable years by the Massachusetts Institute of Technology. The corporation operates over 1,000 training and education facilities and "enrolls" 30,000 employee-students under the 17,000 supervising instructors (Hechinger, 1980). Altogether, Hechinger estimates that in 1978 about 4.3 million employees of America's largest corporations took coursework offered by and within their own companies.

Given the existence of such large-scale educational activity by corporations and other social organizations such as the military and health care agencies, it is not surprising that new ideas concerning education and certification are to be found in the institutions traditionally assigned responsibility for education. Universities and other higher education institutions discovered the proposition that life experience and education gained through activities other than higher education have value, and that these kinds of experiences should be considered by schools and additional organizations for certification (degree) purposes. New ideas, now called nontraditional, include changes in traditional approaches to residential requirements, continuous enrollment, and curriculum and related structured elements of a college degree program.

The acceptance of nontraditional concepts in higher education represents an extremely good example of the interaction between the social context and education. The threat of declining enrollments among the traditional 18- to 22-year-old college-age population greatly facilitated the acceptance of nontraditional concepts. This chapter provides a general discussion of a variety of unconventional ways by which learning is being recognized today. Some of these, such as the continuing education unit (CEU), reflect relicensure procedures rather than original educational entry qualifications for employment. Others, however, are procedures designed to help students obtain degrees. This chapter discusses credit for prior learning through such procedures as (a) national evaluation systems, (b) the portfolio method, (c) external degree programs, and (d) the CEU.

CREDIT FOR PRIOR LEARNING

It can be argued that adults have been "educated" in a number of "schools" other than traditional institutions. Work and other life experiences provide adults with knowledge and skills that may be similar to or different from those obtained in an institution specifically designed as educational. But how does one equate the learning obtained through military service or other training with the educative consequences of one or more college courses? Six kinds of nontraditional procedures for awarding recognition for learning include three national evaluation systems conducted by the American Council on Education (ACE), the College Entrance Examination Board (CEEB), and the Educational Testing Service (ETS) as well as the portfolio method, a variety of external degree programs, and the Continuing Education Unit (CEU).

ACE System

The system adapted by the American Council on Education (ACE) has been used for more than 40 years and is currently the means by which some 2,000 colleges award credit for the coursework students complete in military service. Spielle (1980) reports that in the late 1970s, 164 colleges reported using the ACE guides to award more than 300,000 credits. Even though ACE pioneered its system to recognize military educational experiences, it was broadened to include the rapidly expanding noncollegiate area. More than 500 colleges have introduced the program or a similar one developed by the New York Regents' Program on Noncollegiate Sponsored Instruction to evaluate coursework offered by other sponsors of noncollegiate instruction. Such coursework is offered by business corporations, government agencies, voluntary and professional organizations, and labor unions. Jerry Miller of ACE describes the Noncollegiate Sponsored Instruction project as focusing on instructional systems that have been in place for years and have served their constituents well. Such systems, according to Miller, are very visible and are offered by organizations that are not chartered or licensed educational institutions. The project staff has been engaged in assessing formal learning activities sponsored by such organizations and described as "organizational postsecondary education" (J. W. Miller, 1975, p. 254).

The ACE system is based on four "guides," three for military education and one for other noncollegiate courses. These guides are developed through expert evaluations of each course. The guides provide the course title and number, location, length, and objectives, describe the instruction, and recommend the credit to be awarded.

The ACE program has demonstrated remarkable flexibility and sensitivity to social developments over the years. New program areas under review include application to military occupational specialties and apprenticeship experiences.

College Board System

The College Entrance Examination Board also developed a system to help college and university personnel make decisions about awarding credit. The board provides two major series of examinations: the College-Level Examination Program (CLEP), which contains more than 50 examinations, and the Advanced Placement Program (APP), which contains more than 20 examinations (Valentine, 1980). More than 1,500 colleges use examinations in one of these series, and Florida, Utah, and West Virginia encourage statewide use of CLEP in their higher education systems.

The two examination series serve different populations of students. The CLEP is particularly for adults, and the APP examinations are used primarily by high school students. The major concern of this chapter is with the CLEP adult examinations. Cooperatively, the college board and the ACE have evaluated the CLEP examinations and recommended levels of scores that are appropriate for awarding credit.

ETS System

Several responses have been made to the heightened interest in awarding educational credit for life experience. In 1974 the Carnegie Corporation awarded a grant to the Educational Testing Service, in cooperation with nine colleges and universities, to determine appropriate guidelines and procedures to assess experiential learning. The project staff has been concerned with the development of ways to assess learning that occurs outside of the classroom. The team is also concerned with two aspects of learning as it relates to higher education: learning that has occurred prior to entering an institution of higher education and learning that takes place through the guidelines and sponsorship of a postsecondary institution (Park, 1975). Thus, ETS finds itself engaged in nothing less than measuring, evaluating, and awarding "credit" for life experience.

PORTFOLIO METHOD

The procedures developed by ACE and the College Board are not fully satisfactory. Accordingly, new procedures not based on transcripts, existing examinations, or credit recommendations have been developed. One such approach is the portfolio method.

According to the portfolio method, used at Empire State College in New York, the student works out an individually designed degree program in consultation with institutional faculty. Strange (1980, p. 44) notes that the requirements for a degree at Empire State include the following:

- a minimum of 128 credits
- a maximum of 96 credits in "advanced standing" (credits awarded for principal coursework or experimental learning)
- a minimum of 45 credits in upper-division level coursework
- a minimum of 24 upper-division credits in a selected major
- a minimum of 96 credits (75 percent) in liberal studies for the B.A.; at least 50 percent in liberal studies for the B.S.; or at least 25 percent in liberal studies for the Bachelor of Professional Studies

The candidate's portfolio provides a detailed description of the proposed educational plan, past records or current proposals concerning previous learning to be considered for advanced standing, and outlines of adidtional work planned to meet the remaining requirements. In the final version of the portfolio, other required records such as evaluations for credit, official score reports in support of credit earned by examination, and transcripts covering traditional college courses are included.

When the student and adviser agree that the degree program application and portfolio are complete, the dossier is reviewed by an assessment specialist. The review yields advice concerning items that need strengthening. When approved, the dossier is submitted to a faculty review committee that determines if it meets Empire State College and State University of New York policy requirements (Strange, 1980).

EXTERNAL DEGREES

In the first part of the chapter, some innovative procedures for awarding college credit were discussed. Such procedures may or may not be included in some of the "new" external degree programs that rapidly developed in the United States in the 1970s.

Attempts have been made to define external degree programs more positively. Houle (1973) believes that the general definition is negative because it ultimately says that an external degree is not an internal degree. An external degree is often defined as one that is awarded on some criterion that is not founded on traditional patterns of residential study. Efforts to achieve a more positive conceptualization have resulted in such terms as "adult" degrees and "flexible time/space" (Bailey, 1972). Regardless of the title, the important concept focuses on the modification of requirements concerning administration, instruction, evaluation, and graduation. Modifications in any of these areas may qualify a program as an external degree program.

John R. Valley, perhaps the most informed person in America concerning external degree programs, has developed three classifications of the program. These in turn have been described by Houle (1973):

1. Valley's *administrative-facilitation* model is generally comparable to the extension degree described here. It is one in which a degree-granting instructional institution undertakes "to serve the needs of a different clientele yet . . . holds to its customary degree pattern."
2. His modes of learning model is comparable to the adult degree. Here an institution "establishes a new degree pattern of learning and teaching that seeks to adjust to the capacities, circumstances, and interests of a different clientele" such as adults.
3. Valley's examination, validation, and credits classification includes three models that are refinements of the assessment degree. In the examination model, an institution or agency "which need not itself offer instruction" awards credits and degrees based upon student performance on examinations. In the validation model, an institution, agency, or association evaluates the student's learning "by a variety of means"—not only by examination. The institution essentially restricts its function to that of certification, al-

though it may offer guidance to individual applicants about ways to meet its requirements. According to the credits model, an institution or association "vouches for the quality of student programming" in awarding credits and degrees for work completed elsewhere. One of the best examples of this model is the Council for National Academic Awards of England; the sole formal function of the CNAA is certification through scrutiny of how well other institutions are performing the processes of admission, instruction, and evaluation (Houle, 1973, p. 93).

Discussions of external degree programs therefore may include both nontraditional and traditional approaches to several program elements. For example, the administrative-facilitation model seems to be characterized by procedures through which the institution extends its outreach. Modifications to accomplish the objective may include changes in residence definitions and requirements. This point is illustrated by the institution that maintains its regular admission, curriculum, and graduation policies other than in the area of residence requirements. As a result a student may be permitted to satisfy residence requirements by taking coursework at off-campus locations. This concept may be further modified by changing other elements; for example, telecommunications and computers may be used to replace face-to-face instruction.

At the extreme positions, we may continue to find both the ultraconservative institution that makes no allowance for previous learning and the nontraditional mode that favors a majority of the several different schemes identified with the external degree concept. The latter institution may have no admission requirements and may award credit for life experience through assessment, examination, or portfolio procedures. It may have no set curriculum; it may accept evidence of learning during the program through participation at or in concerts and other cultural activities, in work assignments, through community involvement, and other independently organized and pursued activities. Seldom will one find all of these elements in one program, however. In 1973, Houle concluded that at least one-third of all American colleges and universities were engaged in some kind of unconventional programs. Table 9.1 reports the characteristics of 179 nontraditional undergraduate programs. The table reveals the relative mix of what might be referred to as

TABLE 9.1: Curricular Options or Requirements in Nontraditional Undergraduate Degree Programs

OPTIONS OR REQUIREMENTS	PERCENTAGE OF PROGRAMS[a]	
	Bachelor $(N=112)$	Associate $(N=67)$
Students may begin program at any time (not only start of term)	29	24
Students design own programs	48	13
Most or all of curriculum structured or prescribed	33	66
Learning contracts between students and faculty	42	22
Concentration or major required	51	25
Distribution among courses (general education) required	40	43
Pacing of program individually determined	63	54
Course work at different campuses possible	47	25
Students may earn degree or complete program on part-time basis	60	73
No information	1	0

Note: Cyril O. Houle, *The external degree* (San Francisco: Jossey-Bass, 1973), p. 14. Reprinted with permission.
[a] Special tabulation provided by Janet Ruyle, Center for Research and Development, University of California, Berkeley.

traditional and nontraditional approaches to degree programs.

The evolvement of the patterns of external degree programs took a number of years and a variety of pathways. Such diverse institutions as the University of Chicago, St. John's College in Maryland, Brooklyn College, and the University of Oklahoma blazed new trails in American higher education. Responding to the popular demand for more flexible time and space provisions for earning degrees, a number of institutions have built upon and expanded the earlier efforts. Some of the more prominent programs include those at Empire State College, the University of Oklahoma, Florida International University, and the Extended University of the University of California. The University Without Walls, Nova University, and the New York Regents External Degree programs also enable students to earn external degrees.

The CEU

The previously discussed schemes for awarding recognition for life experience and work-related activities are primarily concerned with relating those activities to college credit. The Continuing Education Unit (CEU), however, is perhaps of more interest to administrators of noncredit adult and continuing education programs. Like the community college, general extension divisions, and nontraditional education programs, the CEU is an innovation that gives higher education a new dimension (Long, 1978).

The CEU emerged from two main sources: learner needs and institutional needs. Learners desired some kind of recognition for their participation in noncredit learning activities. Parallel needs of institutions suggested the value of some mechanism for accounting for the quantity of educational services provided annually. Consequently, the CEU was adopted as a unit to measure the time a learner engaged in a learning activity provided by an agency, organization, or institution. The standard measure adopted defined the CEU as 10 hours of participation. No additional assessment or evaluation was required to determine the quality. The CEU, hence, is a measure of quantity. The interpretation of its value depends on those who desire to accept and recognize it.

The CEU did not come upon the scene without questions and challenges, however. Some pertinent questions relate specifically to the CEU while others are unresolved ones that emerge from the traditional educational scene, such as questions of quality versus quantity, the issues of legitimation or recognition, various responses to the question of accountability, and the topic of formula funding.

It is unlikely that these issues as they relate to either traditional residential degree instruction or the CEU can be resolved here. It is desirable to recognize that the CEU did not alone create or cause the debate on many of the issues. The increasing popularity of the CEU has merely accentuated lack of agreement within the traditional higher education structure.

The CEU is far from being a static concept. Even as this manuscript was being written, a national study of the CEU was in progress. In addition, some of the issues already noted are being addressed in different ways. For example, we now have the "validated" CEU, which is based on some kind of evaluation of the learning activity rather than only the amount of time the recipient devotes to the activity. It seems safe to predict that the CEU will be subjected to a number of different contending social forces that are related to both the more traditional views of education and to the nontraditional views.

A number of factors favorable to the emergence of the CEU can be found in the social forces relating to education and to work. Four such factors are: (a) a widespread public reevaluation of the worth of a college degree, (b) a strong movement toward providing educational credit for life experience, (c) an extended role for education in occupational recertification and relicensure, and (d) the emergence of consumerism coupled with the recognition of professional obsolescence. We will discuss the third factor in this section.

Recertification and Relicensure.   A study by Strother and Swinford has noted an increased emphasis on recertification and relicensure through education.

> The movement toward requiring continuing education for re-certification and re-licensure appears to be more than a flurry. . . . We found that 38 states now have some type of continuing education requirement in one or more of the fourteen professions surveyed. In addition, at least three national groups now require continuing education as a condition for continued membership. (1975, p. 5)

The study also found ambivalence about what constitutes acceptable educational activity, for each of the 14 professions examined appears to have unique definitions of continuing education. Areas of difference include the amount of time devoted to continuing education, the content, and the cost of the experience. According to Strother and Swinford, time requirements, for example, vary from as little as 4 hours per day up to 50 hours of continuing education annually. While many of the professions state their requirements in annual terms, the majority specify that continuing education requirements must be met in a three-year period and must be work-related. The American Medical Association, for example, specifies "accepted sponsorship" for at least 60 of the 150 hours required over a three-year period for the "Physician's Recognition Award." The balance of the continuing education activity can be met through programs of non-accredited sponsors, teaching, writing, individual study, and other meritorious learning experiences.

In most cases, however, the essential question—*who* certifies *what* as acceptable?—remains unanswered. In some states the professional associations are both purveyor and validator. This dual role has raised the conflict-of-interest issue. It can be speculated, for instance, that continuing education requirements conveniently encourage attendance at annual professional conferences and indirectly provide financial incentives for sponsoring organizations. It is also possible that the potential market for continuing education within selected professional areas will stimulate the interest of proprietary organizations in those fields.

SUMMARY AND CONCLUSIONS

We have observed that developments in the broader society are often reflected in educational practice. In this chapter we focused on developments in the certification of learning. In the 1960s and 1970s, educational institutions adopted a number of different strategies to certify learning. The various approaches, from portfolio to CLEP procedures, emerged in response to individual and societal needs. They also reflect other events in the larger society that have contributed to the acceptance of nontraditional approaches to education for adults.

The new procedures are an outgrowth of social developments of the post–World War II era. They also symbolize a dynamic relationship between higher education institutions and other social agencies and organizations. New attitudes toward certification emphasize an important change in educational philosophy: Educational experience is no longer considered limited to coursework taken on college and university campuses. A new "related" educational system has emerged.

The involvement of millions of individuals in military and other noncollegiate education is a conspicuous characteristic of contemporary society. That attitude, when coupled with the rising emphasis on occupational relicensure and/or advancement based on some kind of certified educational activity, is an important factor in the changing relationships between major social institutions such as education, business and defense. Furthermore, this development is also consistent with previously identified characteristics of adult and continuing education in America such as pragmatism, dynamism, pluralism, and creativity. Each of these fundamental attributes of adult and continuing education is discernible in the phenomena described in this chapter.

IMPLICATIONS

Modifications and new developments in recognition of prior learning through experience and other educative activities present adult education organizations with a number of challenges. The developments in nontraditional education contain implications that touch on administrative and organizational areas as well as program delivery, assessment, and evaluation procedures.

It is likely that successful programs in postsecondary areas of adult and continuing education are influenced in some way by the developments noted in this chapter. Other topics discussed in this book, in combination with changes in certifying learning, will continue to be either a threat or opportunity for a number of years.

10 Forecast
and Speculations

This volume is based on the application of four major propositions concerning programming in adult and continuing education:

1. An awareness of larger social issues, events, and trends can be instructive in the program development process.
2. Program planning is informed and rewarded by adherence to historical characteristics of adult and continuing education such as pragmatism, voluntarism, pluralism, and dynamism.
3. Philosophical concerns such as the purpose of adult and continuing education and target audiences to be served interact with variables in each of these two propositions.
4. Programming in adult and continuing education is creative and original.

Within the framework provided by these four propositions, we have discussed social, psychological, and technical developments that have influenced programming recently and may continue to affect it in the future. Some of the social developments that emerged in the last decade, such as concepts of educational equity and entitlements, seem to have encountered resistance that in part can be explained by economic conditions. Thus, as we cast a backward glance over the 1970s, we must also look into the immediate future to discern the outlines of program developments. This chapter is such a speculative venture. It is readily acknowledged that the future is shrouded in a dense mist that obscures events sufficiently that individuals may disagree about the identity of given phenomena.

Speculations concerning some future issues, topics, and trends in programming in adult and continuing education are shared in the following pages. We will discuss: (a) trends and issues identified by Apps, Kreitlow, and Eyre, three leaders in the field, (b) general questions regarding potential developments in some ambiguous areas, (c) potential consequences for programming resulting from selected trends, and (d) thoughts about the future of programs in the field.

TRENDS AND ISSUES

Apps identifies six influences upon adult education in the 1980s: (a) changing population structures, (b) inflation, (c) consumer movements, (d) the status of women, (e) politics, and (f) mixed attitudes toward education (Apps, 1980). Most of these phenomena are also discernible in the more specific items noted by Kreitlow (n.d.) and Eyre (1980), which we shall also discuss. It is instructive to note that Apps's list could be generalized through the use of such terms as (a) demography, (b) economics, (c) social conscience (consumer movement, status of women, and attitudes toward education), and (d) politics (attitudes toward education). Eventually, we can expect that each of the first three general phenomena identified here will be reflected in the fourth, politics, which in turn will have direct or indirect implications for adult and continuing education in the United States.

The general terms cited here are helpful for purposes of analysis. For example, an economic approach is useful in periods of "stagflation," inflation, or depression. Regardless of the terms used to identify a specific economic condition, there is an assumption that the economy is associated with the education of adults in some way that will influence programming. We have already noted one good example of the way the American economy influenced the education of adults in our discussion of the apprenticeship and evening school systems. We found that because able-bodied youths were scarce in the colonies, apprentices were able to obtain much more favorable contracts than could their European cousins. As a result American contracts usually included a clause specifying the apprentice would be taught to read, write, and compute. This provision stimulated the growth and expansion of the evening school movement (Long, 1976).

Even though the contemporary scene is quite complex, some trends likely to influence program content and processes in the immediate future can be identified. Pressure that encourages the development and provision of adult education arises from increasing numbers of participants, rising levels of educational achievement (in terms of years completed), technological change, recertification trends, and demands for management training in business and industry. Responses to these trends also influence the nature of programs, processes used, and institutions engaged in adult education. Kreitlow (n.d.), for example, observes that programs based on self-directed learning skills are increasing. The consequence of such a strategy leads to an emphasis on learner needs, need for home-based resources, and the application of innovative techniques and technology.

Broad social change results in the emergence of issues that must be addressed by society. One way of examining the impact of change and related questions is through adult and continuing education. Some of the major issues that are appropriate topics of educational programming are those related to the following topics (Eyre, 1980):

- economics, inflation, and personal money management
- employment, underemployment, and unemployment
- crime and personal safety
- health and medical care
- conservation, energy, and the environment
- government
- retirement and leisure time
- the family

The social influences, trends, and issues identified by Apps, Kreitlow, and Eyre are not presented as exhaustive. Each author has chosen major social phenomena that represent issues and challenges for adult and continuing education. There is some expected overlap among the four lists. The items cited, along with the content of the chapters in Part II of this volume, also indicate how social events may be multidirectional. Thus, educators cannot always agree on the impact of what may appear to be conflicting trends. Some of the ambiguous trends are discussed in another section of this chapter.

Too little attention, however, seems to have been directed toward a phenomenon that I refer to as the *electronic cottage*. The electronic cottage represents one of the greatest potential threats and/or opportunities to face educators of adults in the last 100 years.

THE ELECTRONIC COTTAGE

The *electronic cottage* is a term that symbolizes the availability of powerful electronic media, as discussed in chapter 4, for education and entertainment. These media can bring into the home information that traditionally was available in limited quantities and quality at external locations. Thus, the electronic cottage is an opera house, research library, simulation laboratory, theater, and computer center.

Developments in the electronic media present one of the most challenging opportunities for adult and continuing education. In a way adult education has experienced a revolution since colonial days. Prior to 1776 few institutions specifically included education of adults among their missions and goals, and much of adult learning was personally organized and pursued. By the twentieth century, a variety of institutions outside the schools had programs primarily designed for educating adults. In the colonial era, it was up to the individual to discover and develop learning opportunities and resources. In the twentieth century, the learner frequently selects from a variety of institutionally developed and structured learning programs designed for groups of adults. However, adults are becoming more sophisticated in self-planned learning.

As the twenty-first century rushes toward us, there is an increasing array of individually pursued learning activities. Computers, television, radio, videotape and videodisc equipment, audio recordings, interactive capability picture phones, "electronic blackboards," and the tremendous variety of available inexpensive print media can convert the most humble apartment into a learning resource heretofore unknown to great scholars. How this electronic cottage will be used, how it will fit into the existing structures for recognizing and certifying learning, is yet unclear. It is very likely, however, that developments in the area of certification, as discussed in chapter 9, will be extended to include the electronic cottage.

The content to be made available through the electronic cottage will include just about anything from classical art, literature, and music to basic automobile and home repair. Public affairs, health, and other topics may acquire a concrete dimension often missing in abstract discussions of political theory and nutrition, for example.

AMBIGUOUS AREAS

The trends and issues identified by Apps, Kreitlow, and Eyre are similar to many of those discussed earlier in this book. They were listed because they succinctly represent the paradoxes that adult and continuing educators face. For example, there is an increasing need for both credit programs and noncredit educational activities for adults. Wider adoption of nontraditional schemes for recognizing and certifying learning is occurring parallel to increasing demand for activities in which people can engage without thought of certificates or credit. Some people want programs designed for personal life enrichment while others emphasize the need for occupationally oriented educational activities. A concern for face-to-face instruction exists simultaneously with the revolution experienced in the electronic media. At a time when the concept of lifelong learning has gained a visibility and acceptance never equalled before, contradicting pressures threaten the financing of such programs. Some propose that adults should bear a greater proportion of their cost while others believe that social conditions make educational programming for adults as much a financial responsibility of the state government as is childhood education (Kreitlow, n.d.).

EDUCATIONAL ACHIEVEMENT

Educational achievement is one of the most significant issues that adult and continuing educators and policymakers must address. During the last decade, a growing concern for relative academic performance has been expressed on a broad front. Numerous articles have addressed the declining SAT, ACT, and GRE scores of American students (Copperman, 1978). Adult and continuing education began its expansion during the "sputnik" era of the late 1950s and early 1960s, when public school curricula were strengthened and when graduating high school seniors began to show rising scores on standardized achievement tests. Such rising scores, however, peaked around 1965, and until 1982 they declined, eventually falling below the level of scores achieved before 1952. Thus, adult and continuing educators who were trained and began their practice between 1965 and 1975 came into contact with young and middle-aged adults who graduated from high school about 1953 and later. These graduates were on the rising slope of the performance curve. In contrast, the younger adults who have entered adult and continuing education activities since 1970 are characterized as being on the downward slope of the performance curve.

Even though educational achievement levels, measured in terms of years of schooling completed, increased between 1969 and 1981, it can be argued that achievement level in terms of ability has declined. Therefore, we find that educational activities today are often based on principles and procedures designed for self-directed learners competent in computation, composition, reasoning, and conceptualizing. The adults now engaged in these activities, being self-directed learners, however, may in fact be students of a different kind. The implications of this very important change are difficult to identify in terms of program planning, but surely adult educators will be challenged in the processes of needs-assessment, identification of appropriate learning resources, and selection of appropriate teaching techniques.

DEMOGRAPHY

The changing demographic profile represents another unsolved puzzle for adult and continuing educators. For example, data on participation patterns indicate that participation is positively associated with educational achievement (years of schooling) and negatively associated with age. Predictions through 2010 indicate that both the average age level and average educational achievement level will increase. Will these two variables of age and educational achievement cancel each other out? Or will educational achievement be stronger than the effect of age? I believe that the educational variable will be the stronger. The strength of the factor, however, may not be as great as some would propose. Furthermore, the effects of other social events and trends may run counter to the educational variable. For example, increasing costs of transportation may erode some of the advantage provided by the rising educational levels.

Scheduling decisions, such as time and place, may also have either negative or positive effects, as may the cost of participation in terms of tuition and other incidentals.

NEED VERSUS DEMAND

Psychologically and socially, the American adult is receiving a number of reinforcements for participating in continuing education activities. Many of these reinforcemnts are identified by Kreitlow (n.d.). The potential *negative* impact of poor learner performance and the reduction in reading ability is difficult to assess. On one hand, it can be argued that the need for remediation will be sufficiently great in the immediate future to stimulate development of strong programs. On the other hand, scholars such as Botsman (1975) indicate that poor educational performance in childhood hinders participation in adulthood, especially for males. Based on these potentialities, it is speculated that although the *need* for adult and continuing education will remain strong, partially because of the decline in basic academic skills, the *demand* for programs may decline, for the potential target audience will associate these programs with prior schooling failure. The picture represented by such a situation is of a society that demands basic academic skills and decision-making abilities that appear to be declining in the general population. The dangers posed by such a situation are numerous and include such catastrophies as governance by an "educational elite."

ENERGY AND ECONOMICS

Energy and economics are two topics of considerable importance in speculating about the future programming in adult and continuing education. The two are intertwined in a complex manner and are therefore difficult to separate. However, some very obvious adjustments in programming have already occurred because of these twin variables. First, more and more, conferences are scheduling Saturdays and Sundays into their calendars. This strategy is directly related to airline fares that are less costly when an individual extends a trip to include Friday or Saturday night. Second, many organizations, as noted in chapter 4, have discovered the teleconference (video or audio only) as a means for conducting training conferences at decentralized locations at only a small proportion of the costs associated with central meetings. Telephone company advertisements regularly compare the cost of a meeting held at a local site through the use of teleconferencing with the cost of a national meeting that includes air travel and two or more days away from work.

THE FREE UNIVERSITY

The nontraditional approaches also contain some conflicts within their structure that must be resolved. For example, universities and colleges are continuing to hold on to the degree-granting privilege or authority. However, as the institutions gradually widen the options for self-directed study and independent learning activities and loosen control over the sources of knowledge they recognize as legitimate, they are also loosening the relationship between the learner and the institution. The concept of the free university is becoming more of a reality. How far will this process go? If the trend continues, what are the implications for colleges and universities that are being placed under increasing pressure to be accountable and to pay a larger share of the costs of an education?

SOME CONSEQUENCES

Given the influences, trends, and issues noted in this book, some potential consequences for programming in adult and continuing education are shared in the following paragraphs. As noted early in this chapter, we can only speculate at this point about consequences, but given the assumptions discussed previously, it appears that the following suggestions are plausible.

1. Institutional pluralism will increase. More, not fewer, agencies, institutions, and organizations will place a greater emphasis on educational programs for adults. More of those institutions, such as hospitals and corporations, that are now primarily interested in internal training will expand their educational programming to include what could be called external markets. The development will lead to increased competition as described in the following paragraph.

2. Competition among the purveyors of adult and continuing education will deepen. The competition will be manifested in several ways. It is predicted that "price wars" and "credential wars" will develop as institutions compete for selected markets. Increased proportions of budgets will be allocated for marketing. Educational institutions will follow the lead of business and profit-making firms by employing a staff of highly trained marketing personnel. Brochure copy and other publicity material will become highly sensationalized, and only institutions with the highest ethics will be able to withstand the temptation to promise more than they can deliver.

3. Increased efforts will be made to attract a larger percentage of the population into adult and continuing education. Institutions and other organizations will attempt to do this through marketing, by providing easier access to credentials of some kind, and by supporting various mandatory education requirements.

4. The second-chance concept will be unevenly accepted in society, at least until the economy improves. Those without a need for remedial education will object to the use of tax funds for that purpose, while those who need such educational opportunity will fail to support programs by adequate participation. In the long run, remediation opportunities will remain a part of adult and continuing education. Expansion of the programs will not be substantial, however, in spite of the speculation concerning the relative deterioration of the average adult literacy level.

5. Institutions will have to be even more creative in their program offerings. Standard bread-and-butter activities that in the past may have had productive lives of several years will diminish in number. New programs with short life expectancy will have to be developed continuously. Developmental costs will thus increase, and adult and continuing education organizations will find it desirable to have fully staffed "research and development" programs that include a variety of programming skills to be interfaced with the marketing division. Programmers will have to work closely with the marketing and technical staffs to develop ways of applying the new electronic media. Criteria will include cost recovery, institutional ownership, educational effectiveness, and popularity.

Programmers in adult and continuing education face a number of profound challenges. To meet these challenges, they must develop skills in interpreting the past and present in order to better predict the future. It is likely that large adult and continuing education operations will develop a special staff of forecasters who spend large amounts of time examining trends such as those mentioned in this book and developing alternative futures based on those analyses.

Adult and continuing educators will need to become better informed about the use of the electronic media, videodiscs, videotapes, slow-scan television, cable television, audiotapes, and computers. Not only will programmers need to know about the technical capabilities of the above media, but they will also be challenged to become better informed about the learning-teaching efficiency of each of the media so that each can best achieve the students' objectives and provide the content they need.

SPECULATIONS

There is little doubt that the future will present exciting and challenging opportunities for adult and continuing education programs. However, there are many reasons to believe that the interaction between American society and adult and continuing education will continue to bring about modifications on both sides. Philosophies of the basic purpose and character of adult and continuing education may prove to be especially sensitive to social trends. Unless they are balanced by a working knowledge of the historical characteristics of the field, abrupt swings in concepts of purpose may result. Structural factors in the environment represent the most fertile area of study for program ideas and design of adult and continuing education. In combination, philosophy of purpose, understanding of historical characteristics, and knowledge of contemporary structural factors in society lead to decisions concerning institutional mission and readiness, interpretation of the environment, needs-analysis, and, consequently, educational program-planning and program implementation processes.

This analysis of the program-planning process in adult and continuing education is too general and broad to permit the application of the model to highly specific predictions of likely program topics. It does, however, suggest some general topics and activities that planners may study within the context of their own mission and target populations. Some of the topics that are likely to be popular during the 1980s are:

1. Secondary health services or preventive medicine
2. Home and automobile maintenance
3. Family concerns
4. Business and management
5. Personal finances
6. Various forms of remediation
7. International topics

Some of these topics may be addressed by a variety of formats. These formats are likely to combine face-to-face instruction with a variety of media. For example, home and automobile maintenance courses may be constructed around shop sessions supplemented by print and broadcast media including the use of home computers for developing trouble-shooting and diagnostic skills. Business management courses can also be enhanced through the combined and integrated use of diverse media including taped lectures and skillfully prepared true-to-life situations. Similar multimedia formats are appropriate for each of the topics in the preceding list. Finally, it is likely that planners will enhance the attractiveness of the learning activities by skillful use of short "units" of instruction that can be mastered according to the needs and schedules of diverse learners.

References
Index

References

Academy for Educational Development. *Never too old to learn*. New York: AED, 1974.

Ackerman, S. P. *Relationship of dogmatism to formal operations* (Doctoral dissertation, University of Georgia, 1978). Dissertation Abstracts International, 1979, *39*(06)3460-A.

Administration on Aging. *Manpower needs in the field of aging*. Washington, D.C.: AA, 1968.

Aker, G. F. *The identification of criteria for evaluating programs in adult education* (Doctoral dissertation, University of Wisconsin). Dissertation Abstracts International, 1962, *22*, 3914.

Aker, G F., Jahns, I., & Schroeder, W. L. *Basic adult education in Coahoma County, Mississippi: An evaluation*. Tallahassee, Fla.: Florida State University, Adult Education Department, 1967.

Apps, J. S. Six influences on adult education in the 1980's. *Lifelong Learning: The Adult Years*, 1980, *3*(10), 4–7.

Arbeiter, S. *Mid-life change: A concept in search of reality*. Paper presented at the National Conference on Higher Education, Washington, D.C., 1979.

Ashford, M. *A comparative analysis of the perceived importance of selected occupational socialization factors to adult educators* (Doctoral dissertation, University of Georgia, 1978). Dissertation Abstracts International, 1979, *39*(8), 4654-A.

Aslanian, C. B., & Brickell, H. M. *Americans in transition*. New York: The College Entrance Examination Board, 1980.

Atlanta Journal Constitution, December 27, 1981.

Bailey, S. K. Flexible time-space programs: A plea for caution. In D. W. Vermilye (Ed.), *The expanded campus: Current issues in higher education*. San Francisco: Jossey-Bass, 1972. Pp. 172–173.

Baker, H. *Retirement procedures under compulsory and flexible retirement policies*. Princeton, N.J.: Princeton University, Department of Economics and Social Institutions, 1952.

Balanoff, N. New dimensions in international media. In P. H. Rossi & B. J. Biddle (Eds.), *The new media and education*. New York: Anchor, 1967.

Baltes, P. B., & Schaie, K. W. Aging and I.Q.: The myth of the twilight years. *Psychology Today*, 1974, *1*(10), 35–40.

Barrett, K. College: Sis-boom-bah-humbug. *Harper's*, October 1975.

Bean, F. P. *Sales and Marketing Management*, n.d.

Bergevin, P., Morris, D., & Smith, R. M. *Adult education procedures*. New York: Seabury, 1963.

Biddle, B. J., & Rossi, P. H. Educational media, education, and society. In P. H. Rossi & B. J. Biddle (Eds.), *The new media and education*. New York: Anchor, 1967.

Bligh, D. Are teaching innovations in post-secondary education irrelevant? In M. J. A. Howe (Ed.), *Adult learning*. New York: Wiley, 1977. Pp. 267–282.

Bonham, G. W. What next? In G. W. Bonham (Ed.), *The communications revolution and the education of Americans*. New Rochelle, N.Y.: Council on Learning, 1981.

Boone, E. J., Shearon, R. W., White, E., et al. *Serving personal and community needs through adult education*. San Francisco: Jossey-Bass, 1980.

Botsman, P. B. *The learning needs and interests of adult blue collar factory workers*. Ithaca, N.Y.: Cornell University Press, 1975.

Boyle, P. G. *Planning better programs*. New York: McGraw-Hill, 1981.

Boyle, P. G., & Jahns, I. R. Program development and evaluation. In R. M. Smith, G. F. Aker, & J. R. Kidd (Eds.), *Handbook of adult education*. New York: Macmillan, 1970.

Brady, H. G., & Long, H. B. Differences in perceptions of program planning procedures. *Adult Education*, 1972, 22(2), 122–135.

Brunner, E. deS., Wilder D. S., Kirchner, C., & Newberry, J. S., Jr. *An overview of adult education research*. Chicago: Adult Education Association of the U.S.A., 1959.

Bryan, W. L., & Harter, N. Studies in the physiology and psychology of the telegraphic language. *Psychological Review*, 1897, 4, 27–53.

Bryan, W. L., & Harter, N. Studies on the telegraphic language: The acquisition of the hierarchy of habits. *Psychological Review*, 1899, 6, 345–375.

Bryson, L. *Adult education*. New York: American Book Company, 1936.

Buchanan, W. W., & Barksdale, H. C. Marketing's broadening concept is real in university extension. *Adult Education*, 1974, 25(1), 34–46.

Burns, T., & Stalker, G. M. *The management of innovation*. London: Tavistock, 1961.

Butcher, L. J. *Free and reduced tuition policies for older students at two-year community, junior and technical colleges*. Washington, D.C.: American Association of Community and Junior Colleges, 1980.

Byrne, J. J. Occupational mobility of workers. *The Monthly Labor Review*, February 1975.

California Postsecondary Education Commission. Using instructional media beyond campus. Sacramento: CPEC, 1979.

Campbell, D. D. *Adult education as a field of study and practice*. Vancouver: Centre for Continuing Education, University of British Columbia, 1977.

Clark, E. H. ABE: To be or not to be? *Lifelong Learning: The Adult Years*, 1980, *4*, 24.

Clarke, M. A. Transitional women: Implications for adult educators. *Adult Leadership*, 1975, *24*, 125–127.

Copperman, P. *The literacy hoax*. New York: Morrow, 1978.

Cortwright, R., & Brice, E. W. Adult basic education. In R. M. Smith, G. F. Aker, & J. R. Kidd (Eds.), *Handbook of adult education*. New York: Macmillan, 1970. Pp. 407–424.

Council of Europe. *Development of adult education*. Strasbourg: COE, 1980.

Cross, K. P. *Accent on learning*. San Francisco: Jossey-Bass, 1976.

Cunningham, P. M., & Veri, C. C. University extension commitment to professionally prepared adult educators: The thirty year old discussion. *Continuum*, 1981, *45*(4), 3–12.

Curtis, J. A. Instructional television fixed service: A most valuable educational resource. In J. A. Curtis & J. M. Biedenback (Eds.), *Educational telecommunications delivery systems*. Washington, D.C.: American Society for Engineering Education, 1979.

DeCrow, R. *New learning for older Americans*. Washington, D.C.: Adult Education Association of the U.S.A., 1974.

Educational Testing Service. *1980 Annual report*. Princeton, N.J.: ETS, 1980.

Elias, J. L., & Merriam, S. *Philosophical foundations of adult education*. Huntington, N.Y.: Kreiger, 1980.

Erikson, E. H. *Childhood and society*. New York: Norton, 1963.

Everitt, J. Mc. *Perceptions of the importance of adult education program planning procedures* (Doctoral dissertation, University of Georgia, 1974). Dissertation Abstracts International, 1975, *35*, 6425-A.

Eyre, G. A. Current issues: Prime time. *Maryland Adult Educator*, 1980, *2*(2), 47–49.

Farmer, J. A., Jr. Professionalization in higher adult education administration. *Adult Education*, 1970, *21*, 29–39.

Faure, E., Herrera, F., Kaddoura, A. R., Lopes, H., Petrousky, A. V., Rahnema, M., & Ward, F. C. *Learning to be: The world of education today and tomorrow*. Paris: UNESCO, 1972.

Ferguson, J. *The open university*. London: University of London Press, 1975.

Ferguson, M. *The aquarian conspiracy*. Los Angeles: Tarcher, 1980.

Florio, C. *Collegiate programs for older adults: A summary report on the 1976 survey*. Paper No. 7. New York: Academy for Educational Development, 1978.

Fowles, D. G. *Estimates of the size and characteristics of the older population in 1974 and projections to the year 2000*. U.S. Department of Health, Education and Welfare, Statistical Memo, No. 31. Washington, D.C.: U.S. Government Printing Office, 1975.

Frandson, P. E. Continuing education for the professions. In E. J. Boone, R. W. Shearon, E. E. White, et al., *Serving personal and community needs through adult education*. San Francisco: Jossey-Bass, 1980.

Glover, R. *Alternative scenarios of the American future—1980–2000* (Ed. Beatrice Gross). New York: Future Directions for a Learning Society, College Entrance Examination Board, 1979.

Gould, R. *Transformations: Growth and change in adult life.* New York: Simon and Schuster, 1978.

Griffith, W. S. Personnel preparation. In H. J. Alford (Ed.), *Power and conflict in continuing education.* Belmont, Calif.: Wadsworth, 1980.

Harrington, F. H. *The future of adult education: New responsibilities of colleges and universities.* San Francisco: Jossey-Bass, 1977.

Havighurst, R. J. Changing status and roles during the adult life cycle: Significance for adult education. In H. Burns (Ed.), *Sociological backgrounds of adult education.* Chicago: Center for the Study of Liberal Education for Adults, 1964.

Hayes, D. Holiday Inn, Inc., Memphis. Personal communication, May 1983.

Hechinger, F. M. Forty years of educational technology. In G. W. Bonham (Ed.), *The communications revolution and the education of Americans.* New Rochelle, N.Y.: Council on Learning, 1980. Pp. 5–10.

Hendrickson, A., & Barnes, R. F. Educational needs of older people. *Adult Leadership,* 1967, *16,* 2–4.

Hiemstra, R. P. Continuing education for the aged: A survey of needs and interests of older people. *Adult Education,* 1972, *22,* 100–109.

Hiemstra, R. P. Educational planning for older adults: A survey of "expressive vs. instrumental" preferences. *International Journal of Aging and Human Development,* 1973, *4,* 147–156.

Holt, M. *Women's programs: A panel presentation.* Paper presented at the meeting of the Association for Continuing Higher Education, Atlanta, Georgia, August 1980.

Horn, J. L., & Cattell, R. B. Age differences in fluid and crystallized intelligence. *Acta Psychologica,* 1967, *26,* 107–129.

Houle, C. O. *The inquiring mind.* Madison: University of Wisconsin Press, 1961.

Houle, C. O. The educators of adults. In R. M. Smith, G. F. Aker, & J. R. Kidd (Eds.), *Handbook of adult education.* New York: Macmillan, 1970. Pp. 109–133.

Houle, C. O. *The external degree.* San Francisco: Jossey-Bass, 1973.

Jain, B. J., & Carl, L. *Comparison of selected Ph.D. and Ed.D. in adult education in North America.* Paper presented at the graduate students' section of the Adult Education Association of the U.S.A., National Education Conference, Boston, 1979.

Johnstone, J. W. C., & Rivera, R. J. *Volunteers for learning.* Chicago: Aldine, 1965.

Jones, L. Y. *Great expectations: America and the baby boom generation.* New York: Ballantine, 1980.

Kindley, M. M. Attacking cancer with subatomic particles. *Smithsonian,* 1981, *12*(7), 80–91.

Knowles, M. S. *The adult education movement in the U.S.* Rev. ed. Huntington, N.Y.: Kreiger, 1977.

Knowles, M. S. (Ed.) *Handbook of adult education in the United States.* Chicago: Adult Education Association of the U.S.A., 1960.

Knox, A. B. *Current research needs related to systematic learning by adults.* Occasional Paper No. 4. Urbana, Ill.: Office for the Study of Continuing Education, College of Education, University of Illinois at Urbana-Champaign, 1977.

Knox, A. B. Administrators. In A. B. Knox (Ed.), *Enhancing proficiencies of continuing educators.* San Francisco: Jossey-Bass, 1979a. Pp. 23–42.

Knox, A. B. (Ed.) *New directions for continuing education: Programming for adults facing mid-life change.* San Francisco: Jossey-Bass, 1979b.

Kotler, P. Strategies for introducing marketing into non-profit organizations. *Journal of Marketing*, 1979, *43*, 37–44.

Kotler, P., & Levy, S. J. Broadening the concept of marketing. *Journal of Marketing*, 1969, *33*, 10–15.

Kreitlow, B. W. *Trends in adult education with implications for vocational education.* Occasional Paper No. 13. Columbus, Ohio: The Center for Vocational Education, Ohio State University, n.d.

Kuhn, S. E. *The relationship of formal operations and syntactical complexity in oral language of adult women* (Doctoral dissertation, University of Georgia, 1978). Dissertation Abstracts International, 1979, *39*(7), 3982-A.

Lawrence, P. R., & Lorsch, J. W. *Organization and the environment: Managing differentiation and integration.* Boston: Harvard University Graduate School of Business Administration, 1967.

Lefstein, L., & O'Barr, J. Peer teaching encounters wide disparity in goals. *Generations* (Western Gerontological Society), Summer 1978, 10–12.

Levinson, Daniel J., et al. *The seasons of a man's life.* New York: Ballantine, 1978.

Likert, R. *New patterns of management.* New York: McGraw-Hill, 1961.

Liveright, A. A. The nature and aims of adult education as a field of graduate education. In G. E. Jensen, A. A. Liveright, & W. Hallenbeck (Eds.), *Adult education: Outlines of an emerging field of university study.* Chicago: Adult Education Association of the U.S.A., 1964.

Liveright, A. A. *A study of adult education in the United States.* Boston: Center for the Study of Liberal Education for Adults, 1968.

London, J. Program development in adult education. In M. S. Knowles (Ed.), *Handbook of adult education in the United States.* Chicago: Adult Education Association of the U.S.A., 1960.

Londoner, C. A. Survival needs of the aged: Implications for program planning. *International Journal of Aging and Human Development*, 1971, *2*, 113–117.

Long, H. B. A summary report: Adult education participation in Brevard County, Florida. *Adult Education*, 1967, *19*[17], 34–42.

Long, H. B. *Participation patterns of the disadvantaged.* Paper presented at the seminar on Teaching the Disadvantaged Adult, University of Georgia, 1970.

Long, H. B. *Psychology of aging: How it affects learning.* Englewood Cliffs, N.J.: Prentice-Hall, 1971.

Long, H. B. Perspectives of the continuing education unit. *Adult Leadership*, 1974, *22*, 268–270, 277.

Long, H. B. The education of girls and women in colonial America. *Journal of Research and Development in Education*, 1975, *8*(4), 66–82.

Long, H. B. *Continuing education of adults in colonial America.* Syracuse, N.Y.: Syracuse University Publications in Continuing Education, 1976.

Long, H. B. The continuing education unit: Background, issues, and nature. In H. B. Long & C. B. Lord (Eds.), *The continuing education unit: Concept, issues and use.* Athens, Ga.: Center for Continuing Education, University of Georgia, 1978.

Long, H. B. Characteristics of senior citizens' educational tuition waivers in twenty-one states: A follow-up study. *Educational Gerontology: An International Quarterly*, 1980a, *5*, 139–149.

Long, H. B. *Historical characteristics of adult education in the United States.* Briefing paper delivered to visiting Chinese adult educators, Belmont, Md., September 1980b.

Long, H. B. How to literature in colonial America. *Lifelong Learning: The Adult Years*, 1980c, *3*, 12–14.

Long, H. B. *Adult learning: Research and practice.* New York: Cambridge, 1983.

Long, H. B., McCrary K., & Ackerman, S. P. Adult cognition: Piagetian based research findings. *Adult Education*, 1979, *30*, 3–18.

Long, H. B., & Rossing, B. E. Tuition waivers for older Americans. *Lifelong Learning: The Adult Years*, 1978, *1*(10), 10–13.

Lord, C. B. Personal communication, September 15, 1980. Lord is Associate Director of the Georgia Center for Continuing Education, University of Georgia.

Luther, J. M., Hendel, D. D., & Mucke, E. E. A program for the continuing education of women looks at its past and plans for the future. *Continuum*, 1981, *46*(1), 1–12.

Marcus, E. E. Effect of age on perception of the utility of participation in education. ERIC, ED 141 691, 1977.

Marin, P. Follies of the human potential movement: The new narcissism. *Harper's*, October 1975, 45–56.

Maslow, A. H. *Toward a psychology of being.* Princeton, N.J.: Van Nostrand, 1962.

Mattran, K. ABE/TESOL: An emerging methodology. In D. Bartley

(Ed.), *The adult basic education TESOL handbook.* New York: Collier-Macmillan, 1979. Pp. 92–99.

McClusky, H. Y. The coming of age of lifelong learning. *Journal of Research and Development in Education,* 1974, 7(4), 97–107.

McClusky, H. Y. Learning opportunities abound. *Generations* (Western Gerontology Society), Summer 1978, 25.

McCoy, V. R. Adult life cycle change. *Lifelong Learning: The Adult Years,* 1977, *1,* 14–21.

McCrary, K. J. *The effects of selected environmental factors on level of cognitive functioning in adults.* (Doctoral dissertation, University of Georgia, 1977). Dissertation Abstracts International 1979, *39*(6), 3303-A.

McGee, P. A. "Merchandising adult education. *Adult Education,* 1959, *9,* 75–79.

Merriam, S., & Mullins, L. Havighurst's adult developmental tasks: A factor analysis. In G. C. Whaples & D. M. Ewert (Eds.), *Proceedings: Lifelong learning research conference.* College Park., Md.: Department of Agricultural and Extension Education, University of Maryland, 1980. Pp. 65–66.

Mezirow, J., Darkenwald, G. G., & Knox, A. B. *Last gamble on education.* Washington, D.C.: Adult Education Association of the U.S.A., 1975.

Michener, J. A. *Centennial.* New York: Fawcett, 1974.

Miller, G. *College and university degrees for the retired and elderly.* Butte, Mont.: Author, 1974.

Miller, J. W. Expanded role of the commission on educational credit of the American Council on Education. *Adult Leadership,* February 1975, *23,* 251–255.

Mirza, M. S. *A study of cognitive structures among adults: Piaget's formal operations stage* (Doctoral dissertation, University of Georgia, 1975). Dissertation Abstracts International, 1976, *36*(12), 7811-A.

Moody, H. R. Education and the life cycle: A philosophy of aging. In R. H. Sherron & D. B. Lumsden (Eds.), *Introduction to educational gerontology.* Washington, D.C.: Hemisphere, 1978. Pp. 31–48.

Morstain, P. R., & Smart, J. C. Reasons for participation in adult education courses. *Adult Education,* 1974, *24,* 83–98.

National Advisory Council on Adult Education. *A target population in adult education.* Washington, D.C.: NACAE, 1974.

National Advisory Council on Adult Education. *A history of the adult education act.* Washington, D.C.: NACAE, 1980.

National Center for Education Statistics. *The condition of education.* Washington, D.C.: U.S. Government Printing Office, 1980.

Neidt, C. O., & Baldwin, L. V. Use of videotape for teaching in-plant graduate engineering courses. *Adult Education,* 1970, *20,* 154–167.

Northcutt, N. *Adult functional competency: A summary.* Austin: University of Texas Press, 1975.

Orem, R. A. *A study of the relationship of teacher social and educational background to selected practices in the adult basic education class-room.* Unpublished doctoral dissertation, University of Georgia, 1973.

Ouchi, W. *Theory Z.* Reading, Mass.: Addison-Wesley, 1981.

Owens, W. A. Age and mental abilities: A longitudinal study. *Genetic Psychology Monographs,* 1953, *48,* 3–54.

Owens, W. A. Age and mental abilities: A second follow-up. *Journal of Educational Psychology,* 1966, 57, 311–325.

Park, D. The cooperative assessment of experiential learning. *Adult Leadership,* 1975, 23, 242–246.

Peers, R. *Adult education: A comparative study.* New York: Humanities Press, 1958.

Perrow, C. A framework for the comparative analysis of organizations. *American Sociological Review,* 1967, 32, 195–208.

Perry, W. *Open university: History and evaluation of a dynamic innovation in higher education.* Milton Keynes, England: Open University, 1976.

Peterson, D. A. Educational gerontology: The state of the art. *Educational Gerontology,* 1976, *1,* 61–73.

Peterson, D. A. Toward a definition of educational gerontology. In R. H. Sherron & D. B. Lumsden (Eds.), *Introduction to educational gerontology.* Washington, D.C.: Hemisphere, 1978. Pp. 1–30.

Peterson, R. E. Present sources of education and learning. In R. E. Peterson, K. P. Cross, J. R. Valley, S. A. Powell, T. W. Hartle, M. Kutner, and T. B. Hirabayashi, *Lifelong learning in America.* San Francisco: Jossey-Bass, 1979.

Piaget, J. *Psychology and epistemology: Toward a theory of knowledge.* Trans. Robin Arnold. New York: Viking, 1971.

Porter, S. Your money's worth. *Athens Banner-Herald,* Athens, Georgia, December 22, 1981.

Pritchard, D. Older adults fail to pursue lifelong learning opportunities. *Generations* (Western Gerontological Society), Summer 1978, 34–35.

Quastel, L., & Boshier R. Educational needs and opportunities as antecedents of job satisfaction. *Adult Education,* 1982, 32(3), 130–141.

Rich, D. Campus offers intergenerational bridge. *Generations* (Western Gerontological Society), Summer 1978, 32–33.

Riddell, B. G. *Psycho-social concomitants of motivational orientation in a group of older adult education participants.* Unpublished master's thesis, University of British Columbia, 1976.

Riley, M. W., & Foner, A. *Aging and society.* Volume 1: *An inventory of research findings.* New York: Russell Sage Foundation, 1968.

Robinson, B. Telephone tutoring in the open university: A review. *Teaching at a Distance,* 1981, 20, 57–65.

Rossing, B. E., & Long, H. B. Contributions of curiosity and relevance to adult learning motivation. *Adult education,* 1981, 32, 27–36.

Royal Commission on the Status of Women in Canada. [Book report.] Ottawa: Information Canada, 1970.

Saindon, J. *Participation of industrial workers in continuing education.* Unpublished doctoral dissertation, University of Georgia, 1982.

Satow, R. Pop narcissism. *Psychology Today,* 1979, *13*(5), 14–17.

Schroeder, W. L. Typology of adult learning systems. In J. M. Peters et al. (Eds.), *Building an effective adult education enterprise.* San Francisco: Jossey-Bass, 1980.

Schwertz, C. *An analysis of the denotations of "program" as employed in ordinary language and adult education discourse, with a typology of program based on the denotations.* Paper presented at the National Adult Association Research Conference, Chicago, 1972.

Seltzer, M. M. Differential impact of various experiences on breaking down age stereotypes. *Educational Gerontology: An International Journal,* 1977, 2, 183–189.

Sheehy, G. *Passages: Predictable crises of adult life.* New York: Dutton, 1976.

Sitek, T. *Midwest Motorist,* November–December 1980, 7–8.

Skinner, B. F. *Beyond freedom and dignity.* New York: Knopf, 1971.

Smith, E., & Martin, Mc. C. *Guide to curricula for disadvantaged adults.* Englewood Cliffs, N.J.: Prentice-Hall, 1972.

Smith, R. L. The communications revolution. In G. W. Bonham (Ed.), *The communications revolution and the education of Americans.* New Rochelle, N.Y.: Change Magazine Press, 1981.

Smith, R. M., Aker, G., & Kidd, J. R. *Handbook of adult education.* New York: Macmillan, 1970.

Spielle, H. Credit for learning gained in military service or employment. In R. G. Moon, Jr., & G. R. Hawes (Eds.), *Developing new adult clienteles by recognizing prior learning.* San Francisco: Jossey-Bass, 1980.

Stanford, E. P. Gerontology education and training: A short history. *Generations* (Western Gerontological Society), Summer 1978, 7–9.

Stern, M. R. Promotion and recruitment of adult students. In C. Verner & T. White (Eds.), *Adult education theory and method: Administration of adult education.* Washington, D.C.: Adult Education Association of the U.S.A., 1965. Pp. 31–36.

Strange, J. Credit for learning gained in life and work experience. In R. G. Moon, Jr., & G. R. Hawes (Eds.), *Developing new adult clienteles by recognizing prior learning.* San Francisco: Jossey-Bass, 1980. Pp. 37–42.

Strolurow, L. M. Programmed instruction and teaching machines. In P. H. Rossi & B. J. Biddle (Eds.), *The new media and education.* New York: Anchor Books, 1967.

Strother, G. B., & Swinford, D. N. Recertification and relicensure: Implications for the university. *Spectator,* March 1975, 5–9.

Sullivan, R. E. Peat, the old world's new energy idea. *Smithsonian,* 1981, *12*(7), 146–157.

Thomas, A. M. The concept of program in adult education. In G. Jensen,

A. A. Liveright, & W. Hallenbeck (Eds.), *Adult education: Outlines of an emerging field of university study.* Washington, D.C.: Adult Education Association of the U.S.A., 1964.

Thorndike, E. L. *Adult learning.* New York: Macmillan, 1928.

Thorson, J. A. Future trends in education for older adults. In R. H. Sherron & D. B. Lumsden (Eds.), *Introduction to educational gerontology.* Washington, D.C.: Hemisphere, 1978. Pp. 203–228.

Titmus, Colin. *Strategies for adult education: Practices in western Europe.* Chicago: Follett, 1981.

Toffler, A. *Future shock.* New York: Random House, 1970.

Toffler, A. *The third wave.* New York: Bantam Books, 1980.

Tough, A. *The adult's learning projects.* Ontario: Ontario Institute for Studies in Education, 1971.

Tough, A. Major learning efforts: Recent research and future directions. *Adult Education,* 1978, *28*(4), 250–263.

Tuckman, B. W. The psychology of the culturally deprived. *Phi Delta Kappan,* November 1967, 29.

Tuckman, J., & Lorge, I. Retirement practices in business and industry. *Journal of Gerontology,* 1952, *7*, 77–86.

UNESCO. *Functional literacy.* Paris: UNESCO, 1970.

U.S. Department of Commerce, Bureau of the Census. *Current population reports, P-20,* No. 206. Washington, D.C.: U.S. Government Printing Office, October 1970.

U.S. Department of Commerce, Bureau of the Census. *Alphabetical index of industries and occupations.* Washington, D.C.: U.S. Government Printing Office, 1971.

U.S. Department of Health, Education and Welfare. *The credit system in colleges and universities.* Prepared for the Office of Education by L. C. Lewis. Washington, D.C.: U.S. Government Printing Office, 1961.

U.S. Department of Health, Education and Welfare. *Opening fall enrollment in higher education.* Report on preliminary survey, 1969. Washington, D.C.: U.S. Government Printing Office, 1969.

U.S. Department of Labor, Women's Bureau. *Fifteen years after college— A study of alumnae of the class of 1945.* Bulletin No. 283. Washington, D.C.: U.S. Government Printing Office, 1962.

U.S. Department of Labor, Women's Bureau. *College women seven years after graduation: Resurvey of women graduates—class of 1957.* Bulletin No. 292. Washington, D.C.: U.S. Government Printing Office, 1966.

U.S. Department of Labor, Women's Bureau. *Continuing education programs and services for women.* Washington, D.C.: U.S. Government Printing Office, 1971.

U.S. Department of Labor, Women's Bureau. *Continuing education for women: Current developments.* Washington, D.C.: U.S. Government Printing Office, 1974.

University of Minnesota, Measurement Service Center, Continuing Education for Women. *Summary of data: Questionnaire and interviews, study assessment and evaluation, continuing education for women.* St. Paul: University of Minnesota, n.d.

Upjohn Institute for Employment Research. *Work in America.* Cambridge, Mass.: MIT Press, n.d.

Valentine, J. Credit for learning assessed by examination. In R. G. Moon, Jr., & G. R. Hawes (Eds.), *Developing new adult clienteles by recognizing prior learning.* San Francisco: Jossey-Bass, 1980. Pp. 29–36.

Verner, C., & White, T. (Eds.). *Adult education theory and method: Administration of adult education.* Washington, D.C.: Adult Education Association of the U.S.A., 1965.

Watts, W. America's hopes and fears: The future can fend for itself. *Psychology Today*, 1981, *15*(9), 36–51.

Wells, R. *How to administer programs for disadvantaged adults.* Englewood Cliffs, N.J.: Prentice-Hall, 1972.

Whatley, L. F. *Expressive and instrumental educational interests of older adults as perceived by adult educators, gerontologists and older adults.* Unpublished master's thesis, University of Georgia, 1974.

White, T. Some common interests of adult education leaders. *Adult Education*, 1956, *6*, 151–161.

Wright, C. R., & Hyman, H. H. Voluntary association memberships of American adults: Evidence from national sample surveys. In R. A. Warren (Ed.), *Perspectives on the American community.* Chicago: Rand McNally, 1966. P. 453.

Wuerger, W. W. Mailing lists—How effective are they? *Adult Leadership*, 1971, 20, 89–90, 113.

Youse, C. F. Promotion and recruitment of part-time students. *Adult Leadership*, 1973, *21*, 246–249.

Index